THE READING TUTOR'S HANDBOOK

A Commonsense Guide to Helping Students Read and Write

by Jeanne Shay Schumm, Ph.D.,
and Gerald E. Schumm Jr., D. Min.

Edited by Caryn Pernu

free spirit
PUBLiSHiNG®

Works
for kids™

The stories of tutors and their students are based on those of real people, but their names and identifying details have been changed to protect their privacy.

Portions of chapters 6–9 have been adapted from *How to Help Your Child with Homework* by Marguerite C. Radencich and Jeanne Shay Schumm (Minneapolis: Free Spirit Publishing, 1997) and *School Power* by Jeanne Shay Schumm and Marguerite C. Radencich (Minneapolis: Free Spirit Publishing, 1992). Used with permission of the publisher.

Library of Congress Cataloging-in-Publication Data
Schumm, Jeanne Shay, 1947-
    The reading tutor's handbook: a commonsense guide to helping students read and write / by Jeanne Shay Schumm and Gerald E. Schumm Jr.; edited by Caryn Pernu.
    p. cm.
    Includes bibliographical references and index.
    ISBN 1-57542-052-X
    1. Reading (Elementary)—United States. 2. Tutors and tutoring—United States. 3. Literacy—United States. I. Schumm, Gerald E., 1947- . II. Pernu, Caryn. III. Title.
    LB1573.S337   1998   98-35086
372.4—dc21   CIP

Cover design by Circus
Book design by Percolator
Copyedited by Betty Christiansen
Index prepared by Kay Schlembach

10 9 8 7 6 5 4 3 2

Printed in the United States of America

Free Spirit Publishing Inc.
400 First Avenue North, Suite 616
Minneapolis, MN 55401-1724
(612) 338-2068
help4kids@freespirit.com
www.freespirit.com

ACKNOWLEDGMENTS

We have many people to thank for their ongoing inspiration. Without them, this book and our love for community involvement would not be.

First, our parents—Ruth and Jerry Schumm, Jim and Vera Shay. From our earliest years, we remember their work with church, scouting, and community action. They are our first and best models.

The Rev. Delbert Gault and Dr. Richard Bailar serve as our professional mentors. From Delbert and Dick, we've learned about the depth of need in our communities—beyond our own comfortable neighborhoods.

Most of all we want to thank the volunteers we've recruited over the years for church, community, and service-learning activities. They've taught us what works—and what doesn't. They've also taught us what a powerful difference one person can make.

A special thanks to Sandra Stroud for her expert help in the original version of our Student Literacy Corps manual used at the University of Miami.

A special word of thanks also to Mary Shay Ellsworth for her expert assistance in research for this book.

We would also like to express our appreciation to the staff at Free Spirit Publishing—they make writing a joy.

CONTENTS

LIST OF REPRODUCIBLE FORMS

INTRODUCTION

Helping students learn to read and write is an important and satisfying undertaking. People decide to devote themselves to this work for a variety of reasons. Sometimes a personal encounter leads people to become more attentive to the needs of others who live so near—but are so far away from our everyday consciousness. This was true for us. For Jerry, his first awareness of the dire needs of individuals in his community came when he first visited a migrant camp as a sixth grader. For Jeanne, the lesson came later when she took her first teaching job and encountered many students from high-poverty areas who could not read or write. For both of us, these experiences are etched in our minds and serve as a constant call to action—a call that has shaped our professional and private lives.

At times, the problems of illiteracy seem so massive that it's hard to imagine what one person could do to make a difference. But events have a graphic way of illustrating the power of individual efforts. When Hurricane Andrew literally slashed and trashed our South Florida community in a few short hours, we felt the shock and the slow understanding of the damage that resulted. Then the work of rebuilding the community began. Individual effort—small acts of concern and kindness—touched lives in ways that most people will never forget. But even more amazing, that individual effort soon became a wave of community collaboration—people from all backgrounds and experiences worked side by side to help and heal. It is like nothing we've ever seen. But it gave us great hope in our community and a true understanding of what individual effort and collaborative cooperation can achieve.

This same combination of individual effort and collaboration is vital in bringing the gift of literacy to all children. And you can be a part. Your individual efforts can combine with those of thousands of others to help stem the tide of illiteracy and bring the gifts of reading and writing to someone in your community.

This handbook draws on our many years of experience in reading instruction, volunteering in our community, and working with volunteers. It's written for tutors who may have little or no experience in teaching reading or writing but do have a strong desire to help others become literate.

Whether you are a volunteer or paid tutor, this book can serve as a valuable resource as you begin your chosen task of helping another person learn to read and write. It can help you find the tutoring opportunity that is right for you, explain some of the features of different types of tutoring programs, and help connect you to the wide range of literacy organizations throughout the United States.

Whether you tutor in a school, library, youth organization, or business, whether you're a student involved in a service-learning project or simply a family member who wants to help, you can use the procedures, forms, and strategies provided in this handbook to enhance your effectiveness as a tutor. You'll learn how to work more effectively with students, parents, teachers, and other professionals to meet your student's special learning needs. You'll discover many ways to make learning more fun. And you'll gain insight on your own strengths and challenges.

Many programs provide little training for tutors, and this book can help prepare you for success. Even if your tutoring program does provide training and materials, this book can give you important background information and insight that will enrich your experience.

ix

These procedures and strategies have been tested and used by hundreds of tutors in Dade County, Florida. Although most of these strategies are most appropriate for tutoring young children and teenagers, they can certainly be adapted for adult learners as well. We've tried to include general strategies that will complement the reading instruction most students receive in school and the wide variety of reading programs you might encounter in community-based programs. You can pick and choose those strategies that best fit your tutoring style and your student's learning needs.

Because many students who are struggling to learn to read are also just learning to speak and listen in English, we've also included tips for tutoring English Language Learners throughout the book. While these obviously won't tell you everything there is to know about teaching English to people who speak other languages, they will help you become aware of some of the special challenges some students face. And they will help you more effectively help your students overcome those challenges.

We appreciate the opportunity to share our ideas with you and hope that you will contact us to share your joys and challenges.

—Jeanne Shay Schumm and Jerry Schumm

> *It suddenly occurred to me that every single thing I worry about—*
> *the breakup of families, drugs, AIDS, the homeless—everything would be better*
> *if more people could read, write, and understand.*
> **— Former First Lady Barbara Bush**

CHAPTER 1

YOU CAN HELP

Raphael Martinez, a college junior, wanted to be a pediatrician. He didn't have much experience working with children, though, so he decided to do something about it: volunteer. "I visited the campus volunteer services office," Raphael said, "and I learned about many ways to get involved with young people—through sports, after-school programs, events like the Special Olympics. But the Student Literacy Corps really interested me. I could set my own schedule. Plus, I'd get to work with students individually, and I'd get academic credit."

Raphael was assigned to work at a local elementary school, where the reading specialist paired him with Jessica, a third grader. "Jessica was so quiet at our first meeting," said Raphael. "She whispered her name. She seemed too nervous to speak, so I started our first two sessions by simply reading stories out loud to her. On our third meeting, she brought me a book to read to her, and she seemed to get over her initial shyness. Now she smiles and laughs and asks so many questions. We take turns reading to each other.

"I'd signed up for only one semester, but I was beginning to see Jessica's progress, and I wanted to work with her longer." So Raphael continued tutoring for another semester. He loved seeing the spark when Jessica caught on to something new.

Through tutoring, Raphael gained confidence in his ability to relate to young people, but he learned more than that. He discovered something extra he could bring to his future patients and their families. "My waiting room is going to have lots of children's books in it," said Raphael. "I'm going to talk with parents about the importance of reading aloud to their children early and often. When I talk with my patients, I'm going to ask, 'Have you read any good books lately?'"

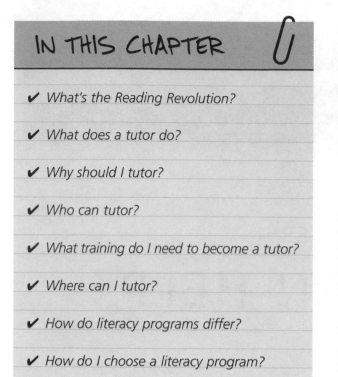

WHAT'S THE READING REVOLUTION?

You've seen it on TV. You've read about it in the newspaper. Everywhere you turn, someone seems to be saying that there's a literacy crisis in the United States—many children aren't learning to read. And many adults don't read well either. A grassroots effort to help children learn to read and write has sprung up among educators, parents, librarians, businesspeople, senior citizens, college students, high school students, and community and religious groups. All these individuals and groups are part of a high-profile national effort to promote literacy, the ability to read and write. Together, they've formed a "Reading Revolution," and anyone can join.

Statistics from the U.S. Department of Education outline the seriousness of the illiteracy problem:

- 40 percent of children are not reading at grade level by the end of third grade.

- 50–70 percent of unemployed adults have minimal or no literacy skills.

- 60 percent of unemployed people lack basic skills needed to be trained for high-tech jobs.

- 60 percent of prison inmates are illiterate.

- 85 percent of all juvenile offenders have a reading problem.

Many children—particularly those growing up in poverty who lack early exposure to reading and adequate preschool experiences—are lagging behind their classmates in reading and writing. Unless they catch up, these students are at great risk for school failure.

Centuries ago, learning to read and write was a privilege of the elite. Only a select few—clergy, scholars, political leaders, the sons of nobility (and rarely the daughters)—were taught. In the United States and other countries, slaves were denied the opportunity to learn to read and write. In fact, teaching slaves to read was against the law. Why? Because literacy is power. The ability to communicate through the written word broadens horizons and opens opportunities that are otherwise closed. As abolitionist author and escaped slave Frederick Douglass said, "A little learning, indeed, may be a dangerous thing, but the want of learning is a calamity to any people."

Times have changed since literacy was a gift for an elite few. Today, most people recognize that the ability to read and write is crucial for success—and not only in school and the workplace. Reading and writing help people communicate with each other, make better decisions about their lives, and respond to challenges. People are justifiably concerned when students don't meet basic standards in reading and writing. When students can't effectively read and write, they also have trouble in science, history, and social studies classes that rely heavily on those skills. As they grow up, they risk not being able to qualify for well-paying jobs, and they miss many opportunities to be fully involved in community life. Schools can't solve the problem in isolation; they need the help of families and other community members.

At least three factors have spurred people to action to deal with the growing literacy crisis:

1. Awareness. In 1983, the much-publicized report of the National Assessment of Education Progress, *A Nation at Risk,* sounded the alert. Since then, the public has become increasingly aware that many students are *not* learning to read and write as they should, and people are looking for ways to help. Although today's students read about as well as students two decades ago, the public better recognizes the need for strong literacy skills.

2. Belief that individuals can make a difference. People are becoming more attuned to the impact that one person can make. National volunteer organizations such as former President George Bush's Points of Light Foundation, retired General Colin Powell's America's Promise: The Alliance for Youth, and President Bill Clinton's AmeriCorps have inspired many people to believe that each of us can make a difference in someone's life. What we do matters.

3. Programs and strategies for people who want to help. Professional educators shoulder the primary responsibility for teaching children reading and writing skills, but parents, volunteers, and others know they can make a tremendous difference in a student's progress as well. Leaders such as former First Lady Barbara Bush and author Maya Angelou emphasize the importance of the simple act of reading aloud to children. The Student Literacy Corps legislation sponsored by Massachusetts Senator Edward Kennedy inspired thousands of college students to get involved in the literacy effort, and in 1998 Congress authorized funding to train thousands of college students to tutor in the public schools. As a result of these efforts, people who have limited or no training as teachers can use specific, effective strategies for helping kids learn to read and write.

Awareness of the dilemma, recognition of the importance of individual effort, and development of systematic ways for motivated people to help teach basic skills—these factors have ignited the Reading Revolution and made it easier than ever before for individuals to get involved.

WHAT DOES A TUTOR DO?

One important way you can become involved in promoting literacy is by becoming a tutor. Tutors play a dual role in their students' lives, offering both instruction and guidance. When you work with a student, you help the student accomplish academic goals, such as improving reading. You also serve as a positive role model, guiding your student in becoming a productive member of society and discovering personal goals. Tutor Aileen Ramos says: "I know my job is to help teach reading and writing to my student, Baxter. But Baxter asks me lots of questions about what it's like to be a college student. No one in his family went to college. In many ways, my job as a role model for Baxter is just as important as my primary job—helping him read."

Tutors also serve as coaches by setting goals with students, encouraging students to meet their goals, and providing structure and support. "I tutor Leon twice a week," says tutor Stephen Tanner. "The time we spend together flies because we're so active. When I'm with him, I really have to be on. He's tried and failed so many times. I have to keep reminding him that he can do it, and prompt and congratulate him all along the way. I feel like a coach, and that's what Leon needs. He needs me to give him direction and encourage him."

WHY SHOULD I TUTOR?

You're obviously thinking about tutoring, even though you may not know fully why you want to do so. People tutor for many reasons: They empathize with people who have trouble reading, they want to share something that's important to them, or they are dedicated to public service. Often the reasons are complex.

You can begin to articulate your reasons for tutoring by writing your own *reading biography*. This is your story of how you learned to read and write and what reading and writing have meant in your life. Reading biographies include stories about mentors who served as role models along the way. They may depict obstacles and triumphs. Some are uplifting and positive; others are stories of pain and self-doubt.

Many tutors share their biographies with their students. Tutor Claudia Hughes says, "When my students see how my handwriting looked when I was younger, it helps them understand that learning to read and write is a process, and you can get better over time." Claudia went all-out, putting together a scrapbook of her experience as a reader and a writer. She included:

- photos of herself reading books

- photos of her teachers

- a photo of an older sister who used to play school with her

- drawings of characters from her favorite books

- samples of her writing from her childhood

- an essay she wrote on learning how to read

Why should *you* tutor? You'll answer that question as you prepare your reading biography. Think of what reading and writing have meant to you. Think about what you can do to bring the joy and power of reading and writing to someone else. Think about what you can do to reduce the pain and self-doubt that difficulties learning to read and write bring to some children.

Reflecting on your early reading and writing experiences can be a powerful way of helping you not only better understand your reasons for tutoring but also remember the struggles and doubts and joys of becoming a reader. Think about how your own experiences might help someone else.

Writing Your Reading Biography

To create your reading biography, think about the questions below and then write your story.

Your biography can be very brief. For examples, see the authors' reading biographies on page 5.

- How did I learn to read and write?

- When did I learn to read and write?

- Who was most helpful in teaching me to read and write?

- What are my first memories of stories and books?

- Was learning to read and write easy or difficult for me?

- If learning to read and write was difficult, how did I feel? How did I cope?

- If learning to read and write was difficult for someone close to me, how did he or she feel? How did he or she cope? How did I feel about this person's difficulties? How did I cope?

- How have reading and writing helped me over the years?

- Why do I want to help someone learn to read and write?

Jeanne's Reading Biography

Mom and Dad were my first and best teachers. Mom was patient enough to read the same books to me over and over. I wanted to be an actress, so she read and reread poetry to me so I could memorize my lines. She also joined a book and record club so that I could listen to the records as I read along. It seemed Mom was always there to read to my brothers, my sister, and me.

Dad took us to the library every week—the Carnegie Library in South St. Louis with its big white columns and lots of steps. I always imagined that Dad was taking me to a wonderful and magical place where each week I could receive a "gift": books to treasure and relish all week long.

I don't even remember "learning" how to read and write. It just happened. I even dreamed someday of becoming a writer, just like Louisa May Alcott.

The realization that learning to read and write wasn't that simple for other people came when I started teaching. My first class in North Carolina included forty sixth-grade students—all reading far below grade level. This was the class for students with learning problems. The other sixth graders called them "Schummie's Dummies." It was my first year of teaching and our first year of marriage. I came home every night and cried because I just didn't know what to do to help. I promised myself I'd spend my career helping students who needed the most help.

Jerry's Reading Biography

I grew up on Singer Island in Palm Beach County, Florida, with my older sister and three younger brothers. We lived just a block and a half away from the Atlantic. Most of our time was spent outdoors swimming and fishing.

Both Mom and Dad worked full time outside the home. My dad sold newspaper advertising and my mom was a nurse. When they were home, however, they focused on family. They cooked, cleaned, shopped—really worked together to keep our family of seven functioning. Dad also was a scoutmaster and a coach for our

baseball teams. Reading wasn't a typical family activity. It seemed like there were too many other things going on.

We didn't have public kindergarten, so my formal education began when I was seven. I remember learning to read in school during reading groups using Alice and Jerry books (Dick and Jane didn't reach southern Florida). We didn't have a public library nearby. But with so many things to do outside all year long, who cared about sitting down with a book?

I admit I don't consider reading or writing pleasurable activities. They seem like necessary communication skills to me. I didn't want to help people learn to read and write so they would "love" it. I think of reading and writing more pragmatically. Some love to read and write; others read and write because it's necessary in our society. My goal is to help people get a decent education, compete for jobs, and otherwise function in our economy.

Your reasons for becoming a reading tutor are personal and deserve to be respected, but remember that there are limits to what tutors can accomplish. Here are some "reality checks" for potential tutors:

You can't create miracles overnight. For many people, learning to read and write is a long process. Remind yourself that individuals learn at different paces and in different ways.

You can't teach someone to read and write all by yourself. You won't be working in a vacuum when you tutor. You'll be working with parents, classroom teachers, and other professionals. Collaboration and communication are your most important allies.

You probably won't teach your student to care about reading and writing in the same way you do. People have different purposes for reading, different likes and dislikes in what they read, and different reading habits. Accept and respect these differences.

WHO CAN TUTOR?

People of all ages and from all walks of life become tutors: teachers, business people, retirees, parents, high school students, and college students. You don't need professional training to use the many powerful strategies that promote reading and writing. Any caring person who wants to offer his or her time and talent can help someone learn to read and write.

You can choose among many different programs to find one that fits your background, goals, and personal style. Tutors can be paid for their time, or they can volunteer. They can tutor full time or part time. They can have extensive or minimal training. Here are some of the possibilities:

Paid Tutors

Professional tutors. Some tutors provide private services at reading centers or in homes. Others work for independent businesses or national chains, such as the Sylvan Learning Centers. The background and training of professional tutors range considerably. Some tutors have very little training; others have teaching degrees. Some even have advanced certification in special education or reading. Such specialists can provide intensive help to students who have severe difficulties learning to read and write.

Paraprofessionals. Also called teacher aides, paraprofessionals serve in support roles in schools. They may work part time or full time. Many schools hire people without teaching certification to tutor students under the supervision of a teacher or reading specialist.

Student workers. Some students are paid to tutor, usually by the hour. For example, the Reading Excellence Act provides federal work-study money to college students who tutor schoolchildren.

Volunteer Tutors

Affiliated volunteers. Many unpaid volunteers are associated with a nonprofit organization, such as a congregation, sorority or fraternity, or service organization. For example, the Phi Theta Kappa national honor society for community college students makes literacy a priority, and its members frequently volunteer in literacy efforts.

Corporate volunteers. Many businesses encourage employees to volunteer, and some even require it over and above regular job responsibilities. The New York–based Everybody Wins! Foundation, for example, runs the Power Lunch program, which encourages adults in business and industry to read books to children over the noon hour.

Service-learning students. Students in middle school, high school, and college often tutor as part of a course or community service requirement. For example, at Washburn High School in Minneapolis, Minnesota, ninth-grade and tenth-grade students can meet their service-learning requirements by tutoring children at an adjacent elementary school.

Independent volunteers. Individuals regularly donate their time and effort to literacy initiatives. For example, community members may contact their neighborhood schools and offer to work with children in a classroom or in after-school programs.

Family members. Parents, guardians, grandparents, and even friends may serve as reading tutors. Tutoring sessions may be formal, scheduled during a special time each week, or informal, taking place as needed.

Flexible volunteers. Many people can't make a regular commitment to tutor but want to be involved on some level. Many cities have clearinghouses that connect people with agencies that offer opportunities that fit volunteers' schedules. For example, D.C. Cares links volunteers with agencies throughout the Washington metropolitan area.

Hundreds of thousands of people across the country have become tutors. And as you can see, there are many ways to become involved.

WHAT TRAINING DO I NEED TO BECOME A TUTOR?

Because volunteer tutoring programs vary so widely, they each have different training requirements for tutors. Several factors determine the training you'll need:

The program you choose. Some tutoring programs require intensive training; others don't. Some are very structured and require little planning from volunteers; others take more forethought. Six types of programs are discussed more fully on pages 7–9, under the heading "How Do Literacy Programs Differ?"

The roles and responsibilities you'll have. If you're going to read aloud to a first grader, you probably won't need much preparation. If you're going to provide intensive, systematic instruction, you'll need more training.

Your background and experience. If you've had previous tutoring experience or you've taken some education courses, you'll need less training.

You should receive enough training to be comfortable in your role. Your training should also make clear what you're trained to do and what you're not. Realize your limitations and ask your tutor coordinator where to go for additional support and expertise.

WHERE CAN I TUTOR?

Tutoring opportunities are popping up all over the United States. To find an opportunity that suits you, start looking in some of these places:

Public schools. Public schools usually offer volunteer and paid tutoring opportunities both during and after school hours. Call a school in your neighborhood or your school district office. Many school districts have a volunteer services office that coordinates tutoring and training opportunities.

Nonprofit agencies. Religious institutions, Boys & Girls Clubs, YMCAs and YWCAs, the United Way, and other nonprofit agencies often offer after-school and weekend tutoring opportunities. Check in the Yellow Pages under "Associations" to get some leads.

Public libraries. Public libraries regularly serve as meeting places for tutors and students. Call or visit your local library to find out more about programs that are available.

You can also check your local newspaper regularly; many daily and weekly newspapers list local volunteer opportunities and information about tutoring programs. The national programs listed under "Check It Out" on pages 10–11 may also help you find local opportunities. For ideas on how to approach any of the potential leads you collect, see "How Do I Choose a Literacy Program?" on page 9.

HOW DO LITERACY PROGRAMS DIFFER?

When you are looking for a volunteer opportunity, it helps to know more about the many different options available. Understanding the structure and goals of different programs can help you find an opportunity that fits your needs and goals. Programs generally follow one of six models: literature-centered, schoolwork-centered, materials-centered, professional-centered, tutor-centered, or a combination of these.

Read to Them, Please: Literature-Centered Programs

Literature-centered programs focus primarily on reading aloud. As you'll discover in Chapter 6, reading aloud with a student has many academic and social benefits. Training for these programs typically includes tips for reading aloud and suggestions for choosing appropriate books. For example, the Kiwanis Club's Raising Readers program in Biscayne Bay, Florida, enlists volunteers from the business community to read aloud to students once a month in public schools. All tutoring occurs in the school's media center, and the media specialist and school counselor help volunteers select books for the read-aloud sessions.

Help with Homework: Schoolwork-Centered Programs

Many after-school programs focus on schoolwork. In these programs, students bring their homework to the tutoring site, where tutors help them complete assignments. For example, the Boys & Girls Clubs provide a "study hall" for youth who attend their after-school program. Trained volunteers at the study hall help students with their assigned work. These programs train tutors to provide support and encouragement without actually doing the students' homework.

Just Follow the Book: Materials-Centered Programs

Publishers, professional organizations, and school districts are beginning to develop structured programs that include specific materials for volunteer and paid tutors. These materials are designed so tutors can follow the program easily with little preparation. Training typically focuses on the procedures described in the materials and often includes role-playing tutoring sessions. In the America Reads program, for example, reading supervisors in the Miami school district have developed a set of tutor-training materials and instructional materials for students in first grade. This highly structured program includes repeated readings of children's stories, practice with word recognition, and writing activities. Tutors receive intensive instruction and supervision from professional staff who have also been trained in the program. The instructional activities and record-keeping system are highly scripted, and tutors are encouraged to follow the program closely.

Let the Pro Be Your Guide: Professional-Centered Programs

Professional-centered programs rely less on materials and more on the judgment of a professional, such as a special education teacher or reading specialist. The professional assesses the student's challenges in reading and writing and then provides the tutor with materials and activities to address those challenges. Training for these programs usually includes an orientation to procedures coupled with ongoing training on specific materials and methods. For example, teachers may plan an after-school program and supervise parent and student volunteers from a local high school. The teachers plan activities for individual students based on their identified needs. The tutors then work with students one-to-one to complete the activities.

Do Your Own Thing: Tutor-Centered Programs

Tutor-centered programs leave tutors to their own devices to assess student needs and select materials to help students overcome challenges. Because these programs provide little support, they're usually best for tutors who have some background as educators, such as retired teachers or education students. For example, Betty Kilbride was an elementary school teacher for thirty-five years before she retired. She now volunteers two days a week at a local school, tutoring children with reading problems. Betty works with relatively little guidance because she is familiar with the school's curriculum and is skilled in identifying students' needs.

Mix and Match: Combination Programs

The previous five models are not mutually exclusive. Many programs combine different elements of these models. For example, in the Student Literacy Corps program at the University of Miami, tutors are trained to use read-aloud techniques (literature-centered model), help students with their homework (schoolwork-centered model), and collaborate with professionals at the tutoring site (professional-centered model). They are also trained in a variety of reading and writing strategies so that they can "do their own thing" if the coordinator at the tutoring site does not have assignments for the student to complete (tutor-centered model).

HOW DO I CHOOSE A LITERACY PROGRAM?

Because so many different programs are available, deciding which program is right for you can be confusing. Just the process of calling to get information about programs can be bewildering, so when you begin your research:

- Be prepared for answering machines. Some agencies are understaffed or have limited hours.

- Be prepared to talk with someone who may not have answers to your questions. In some cases, volunteers who answer the phones don't have detailed information on all programs. In other cases, school secretaries need to refer your call to the teacher or reading specialist in charge of tutoring.

- Be prepared to play "telephone tag" for several days. When leaving a message, it's best to leave specific days and times when you will be available for a return call.

- Be prepared to tell a little about yourself and why you want to become a reading tutor.

- Be prepared to ask questions that will help you screen the tutoring site and see if it might meet your interests and needs. (See the box on this page for some helpful questions to use during an initial phone screening.)

- Be persistent and patient. If people don't call back, or if you can't get all the information you want and need on the first call, it doesn't mean that the school or agency isn't interested in you. Many schools and agencies are under-

funded and understaffed—that's why you are needed so desperately. Give yourself enough time to gather information.

Questions to Guide Telephone Screening of Tutoring Sites

1. *Are tutors paid or volunteer?*

2. *How old are the students involved in the program?*

3. *How many hours a week should I expect to spend tutoring?*

4. *Do you ask tutors to agree to a certain length of service? If so, how long?*

5. *Where does the tutoring take place?*

6. *What type of training do you offer tutors?*

7. *What commitment does the training require?*

Once you've made initial contact with a number of schools and agencies, you can narrow down your options. Which opportunities seem to best fit your schedule, skills, and goals?

Before you commit to a particular program, consider conducting a more in-depth screening. When you choose a tutoring program, you're giving generously of your time and efforts. By planning your decision carefully, you can better ensure that you'll find the right program for you. This second layer of screening can include a visit to the tutoring site, an interview with the tutor coordinator, and perhaps an opportunity to talk with other tutors or families involved in the program.

Your goal is to learn more about the purpose of the program, the leadership and stability of the program, and the satisfaction of students and their parents. Make sure you're able to confirm the details you discussed over the phone, and ask about other things that might help you decide. For example:

- What is the mission of this program? What need does it fill in the community?

- How is this program different from others?

- Who are the program leaders? What are their skills and training?

- What kind of ongoing support does the program have for new tutors?

- What equipment and materials are available?

- How long has the program been in place?

- How long do tutors usually stay with the program?

- What do students like about the program? What do they dislike?

Your visit and questions should help you see how well the program is run and whether it seems to be a good fit for you. After your visit, ask yourself some questions:

- Does the program provide me with the support I need?

- Are my responsibilities clear?

- Am I comfortable with my role and the people I'll be working with?

- Is the tutoring site convenient for me?

- Are the hours convenient?

You can also ask to observe a tutoring session or volunteer for a brief trial period before you make a decision, or compare this opportunity to others. After that, the decision is yours.

Check It Out

Hundreds of organizations are working to promote literacy. Here are a few of the major organizations and inititatives that provide resources and services across the United States.

America Reads Challenge
600 Independence Ave. SW
Washington, DC 20202
1-800-USA-LEARN (1-800-872-5327)
http://www.cns.gov/areads/

The America Reads Challenge is a nationwide program designed to help students throughout the United States learn basic reading skills. The Challenge has initiated summer programs (Read*Write*Now!) and has launched legislation to promote programs for children. One of the most comprehensive programs has been the America Reads Federal Work-Study program. Thousands of college students have been hired as tutors in schools and community agencies. America Reads also includes the Prescription for Reading Partnership that encourages pediatricians to "prescribe" reading to their clients.

American Library Association
50 East Huron St.
Chicago, IL 60611
(312) 280-2162
1-800-545-2433
http://www.ala.org/ala_id/what.html

The American Library Association has a long history of promoting access to information for all citizens. Many libraries across the United States serve as centers for tutorial programs. The association has a catalog with materials promoting reading and literacy. Many of the materials (bookmarks, posters, etc.) are relatively inexpensive and can be used with your students.

Barbara Bush Foundation for Family Literacy
1112 16th St. NW, Ste. 340
Washington, DC 20036
(202) 955-6183
http://www.barbarabushfoundation.com/

The Barbara Bush Foundation's primary purpose is to promote literacy in the home—the child's first place of schooling. The Web site and other publications provide information about effective family literacy programs and procedures, as well as literacy initiatives throughout the United States.

Everybody Wins! Foundation
165 East 56th St.
New York, NY 10022
(212) 832-3180
fax: (212) 832-3965

The Everybody Wins! Foundation was founded in 1991 by Arthur Tannenbaum. This nonprofit organization promotes reading among children so that they can succeed in school and in life. The foundation's primary program is the Power Lunch (a read-aloud program matching young children with adults from business and industry).

Laubach Literacy, Inc.
1320 Jamesville Ave.
P.O. Box 131
Syracuse, NY 13210
(315) 422-9121
http://www.laubach.org/

Laubach Literacy, Inc., was started in 1955 to provide support for adults in learning to read, write, and compute. This nonprofit, volunteer-based organization has over 1,000 sites nationwide. The Laubach training materials are designed specifically for adults, and tutors are provided with systematic instruction in using the materials.

Phi Beta Sigma Fraternity
145 Kennedy St. NW
Washington, DC 20011
(202) 726-5424

Chapters of the Phi Beta Sigma fraternity perform on-site tutoring, primarily with elementary school students having difficulty learning to read. Approximately 60 percent of the chapters across the United States are now engaged in tutoring efforts.

Reading Is Fundamental (RIF)
Dept. WB
P.O. Box 23444
Washington, DC 20026
(202) 287-3220
http://www.si.edu/rif/books.htm

RIF is a nonprofit organization promoting children's literacy. RIF has a network of volunteer-run programs that focus on distributing books to children and making reading fun for children through exciting reading-related activities.

Student Coalition for Action in Literacy Education (SCALE)
Campus Box 3505
University of North Carolina—Chapel Hill
140-1/2 East Franklin St.
Chapel Hill, NC 27599
(919) 962-1542
http://www.unc.edu/depts/scale/mainpage.html

SCALE is a national organization that enlists college students to serve as literacy ambassadors in community service organizations. SCALE membership includes college students, faculty, and administrators. The national office organizes training and technical assistance for members working as reading tutors.

A B C D E F G H I J K L M N O P Q R S T U V W X Y Z

I want every American to say, "What can I do?" Not, "What can I do for the neighbor who looks just like me?" but "What can I do for a lad who is hurting and needs me to come across town and put myself out?"
— **Retired General Colin Powell**

CHAPTER 2

GETTING STARTED

Imagine you're a first grader sitting in a classroom with thirty-five other students. You've just moved, not only to a new school, but to a new city and country in which you know no one outside of your family and you speak no English. In school, you can't understand one word of what's going on. You sit and color pages in a phonics workbook while the other children not only enjoy lessons and classroom activities, but talk to each other and understand what their teacher is saying. For you, the classroom is filled with gibberish and strangers. That's what school was like for Maria Elena, who was new to learning English.

Now imagine that one day a week an enthusiastic young college student comes to visit you—to talk with you; to read stories to you; and to teach you to speak, read, and write English. Imagine how excited you'd be about the weekly visits. That's what happened to Maria Elena when Diana Morris became her tutor. Suddenly, she not only had a friend— someone who clearly cared about her and wanted to make sure she felt comfortable in her strange new circumstances—but a key to understanding and learning a new language. Maria Elena looked forward to Diana's Wednesday visits; each week she wore her prettiest dress and her best patent-leather shoes. Diana's visits were a ray of sunshine, a beacon of hope for a little girl struggling to belong in a new school and a new country.

IN THIS CHAPTER

✔ Your responsibilities as a reading tutor

✔ Your rights as a reading tutor

✔ Ready, set, go!

You understand the pressing need to help children become confident, competent readers and writers. You've heard the call and are ready to help at least one person know the joy of communicating through the written word. But before you say yes to a tutoring commitment, you need to develop realistic expectations about the experience. You need to understand your responsibilities and rights.

YOUR RESPONSIBILITIES AS A READING TUTOR

When you agree to become a reading tutor, you are making a commitment to a child's education. Obviously, details about a reading tutor's role and responsibilities will vary among programs, but a reading tutor has five general responsibilities.

The Tutor's Responsibilities

1. You have the responsibility to be there when you say you will.

2. You have the responsibility to get to know your student, especially your student's strengths and challenges as a learner.

3. You have the responsibility to support and encourage your student.

4. You have the responsibility to plan, implement, and evaluate tutoring sessions.

5. You have the responsibility to communicate in positive and productive ways with key stakeholders (for example, parents and teachers).

1. You have the responsibility to be there when you say you will.

We all like personal attention. We enjoy being around someone who cares for us, cares about our learning, and listens to what we say. Your student, then, will look forward to your tutoring sessions and miss you if you aren't there. Think about Maria Elena—her tutoring sessions with Diana became the highlight of her week.

The staff at your tutoring site also depend on your visits. The trait most tutor coordinators value above all others is dependability—tutors who are there consistently and on time. As one tutor coordinator said, "We don't need more fly-by-nights; we need people who will be there."

Here are some steps you can take to ensure your dependability as a reading tutor:

Set a realistic schedule. Choose dates and times for tutoring sessions that are convenient for you. Remember to plan for travel time to the tutoring site. Many people start by tutoring a few days and hours at a time and then build to a larger commitment. Overcommitting at the beginning might lead you to backtrack and cut down on hours later. Once you've agreed to times and dates, people will be relying on you, especially your student. Choose a few convenient dates and times and go from there.

Arrange for a trial period. To make certain that your tutoring schedule and responsibilities are manageable, arrange for a trial period of three to four weeks. At the end of the trial period, meet with the tutor coordinator to evaluate the experience and to determine how long your service will last—perhaps a semester or a year.

Arrange times for periodic reviews. You can always renew or extend your commitment, but setting a specific length of service and arranging for periodic reviews to see how things are going will benefit you and the program as a whole. Reflection and evaluation can make your tutoring more effective.

Inform the tutor coordinator when you need personal time. You'll need time for vacations, holidays, and other special events. If possible, let your tutor coordinator know in advance (and in writing) when you will be away. Also, let your student know well ahead of time when you will be away.

Ask about procedures for calling in sick. Of course you won't meet with your student when you're ill, so be sure you understand what to do on those occasions. Ask if you need to leave emergency plans for the tutoring session if you are ill or otherwise unable to come at the appointed time. If you find yourself calling in frequently with last-minute excuses, it may be time to reevaluate your commitment.

You are the key to the success of your tutoring sessions. *You* are the key to helping your student become a successful reader and writer. Therefore, your most important responsibility is to be there—regularly and on time.

2. You have the responsibility to get to know your student, especially your student's strengths and challenges as a learner.

Tutoring sessions are highly individual encounters. One size does not fit all. One of the true joys of tutoring is getting to know your student. Focus on your student's strengths and tackle challenges one small step at a time. It will be a growth experience for your student—and for you.

Notice the emphasis on strengths and *challenges* rather than strengths and *weaknesses*. The word *challenge* offers hope. Throughout this book, you'll learn how to build on your student's strengths and help your student cope with and overcome challenges. In Chapter 3, you'll read about students with special needs and the specific challenges some students have in learning to read and write. You'll also learn how to get information about your student by collaborating with parents, teachers, and others who have a stake in your student's success. If you work with students who are learning English, pay special attention to the Tips for Tutoring English Language Learners that you find throughout this book.

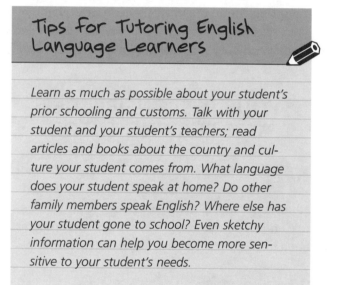

Tips for Tutoring English Language Learners

Learn as much as possible about your student's prior schooling and customs. Talk with your student and your student's teachers; read articles and books about the country and culture your student comes from. What language does your student speak at home? Do other family members speak English? Where else has your student gone to school? Even sketchy information can help you become more sensitive to your student's needs.

One of the most vital sources of information about your student is your student. Of course, the most important thing to learn is your student's name—what he or she likes to be called and how to pronounce it correctly. (Chapter 5 includes guidelines for your first meeting and suggestions for learning about your student's interests, preferences, goals, and challenges.) You'll learn a great deal about your student during the first meeting, and you'll continue learning more about each other if you make the effort.

3. You have the responsibility to support and encourage your student.

David is in fifth grade. He reads on a first-grade level. He's bright—gifted, as a matter of fact—but he also has a learning disability that has prevented him from learning to read and spell. David has a history of failure in school, and he's now afraid to try and to take risks.

Many students who aren't succeeding at reading have tried, like David has. What they need is specific, intensive, individual instruction in reading. But more than that, they need specific and frequent support and encouragement, and you can provide that.

Many students who have difficulty in school have high self-esteem in other areas. They may feel very good about their friendships, their athletic performance, their music ability, or their relationships with family members. Most, however, do not feel good about their work at school. They've learned that school is not a comfortable place to be; it's not a place where they can succeed.

The best way for students to improve their academic self-esteem is by improving in academics. In other words, for students to feel better about themselves as readers and writers, they need to learn to read and write.

As a tutor, you can offer frequent, specific words of encouragement about academic achievements. Focus on the learning. For example, it is better to say, "Pam, that's great! You were able to read six new words today!" than, "Pam, you're a great kid." Ongoing reminders about specific achievements, even seemingly small ones, can build a student's academic self-esteem, slowly but surely. (See the box on this page.) Chapter 4 discusses tangible rewards for your student—what types of rewards are most appropriate, and when.

Encouraging Words*

Words of Acceptance
- *You really seem proud of yourself for figuring that out*
- *What do you think you could do to feel better about it?*
- *You seem frustrated. Try it this way.*
- *You seem to really feel good about that.*
- *I really like working with you because...*

Words of Appreciation
- *I really appreciate your...*
- *That was nice of you to...*
- *That was great, the way you...*

Words That Show Confidence
- *Keep going; I know you can do it.*
- *I have confidence in you because...*
- *I know this is hard, but you'll figure it out.*

Words That Recognize Effort and Improvement
- *In just one week you learned...*
- *Look how much you have improved.*
- *You really worked hard on that!*
- *Yes, you got some wrong, but look how many you got right!*

4. You have the responsibility to plan, implement, *and* evaluate tutoring sessions.

The heart of any tutoring session is the time you spend with your student. But time spent tutoring is only part of the picture and part of your responsibility as a tutor.

---

*Used with permission from the "Coca-Cola Valued Youth Program Tutor Workbook" by the Intercultural Development Research Association (San Antonio, 1991).

Each tutoring session can be divided into three parts:

Before the session, you need to plan objectives and activities and gather your equipment and materials. As you'll learn in Chapter 4, the amount and type of planning you do depend on how the tutoring program is structured. In any case, sessions will run more smoothly if you plan each session and prepare yourself—physically and mentally—for the time you'll spend with your student.

During the session, you need to give your student your undivided attention, follow your lesson plan, and adjust your plan as needed. Chapter 5 offers some tips on setting the tone for tutoring sessions. Chapters 6–8 introduce a variety of strategies you can use to teach reading and writing. Chapter 9 provides additional suggestions for making the sessions lively and fun—for your student and for you.

After the session, take time to reflect. Evaluate the session on your own, but include your student, too. What did the student like or dislike? What worked for the student and what did not? Reflect on successes—big and small. Reflect on challenges—what can you improve for future sessions? Reflect on areas where your student needs additional attention and support. Chapter 10 provides specific suggestions for evaluating tutoring sessions and for helping you learn and grow as a tutor.

5. You have the responsibility to communicate in positive and productive ways with key stakeholders (for example, parents and teachers).

Once you start tutoring, one of the questions you'll be asked most frequently is, "How's it going?" You'll also be asked questions like, "Is Ricky doing better with his reading?" "Is Plo's writing getting better?" "What is Francisco's reading level now?"

Key stakeholders are the people who have a vested interest in your student's progress in reading and writing: organizers and coordinators at your tutoring site, your student's parents or guardian, and your student's classroom teacher (whether or not you are tutoring at the school). Many people may ask about your student's progress, but before you answer, you should know the following:

■ Who is entitled to information?

■ When and where should information be shared?

■ How should information be presented?

Who is entitled to information? Find out whom you are supposed to communicate with regarding your student's progress. For example, should you talk with your student's parents or guardian, the school principal, or your tutor coordinator?

Also find out about your tutoring program's policies on confidentiality. In general, don't talk about your student with anyone other than designated stakeholders. This guideline isn't as easy to follow as it seems, and violating confidentiality can lead to prickly situations. Consider the following example:

B.J. was a volunteer tutor for Scott in a high school reading remediation program. He met Scott's mom through a chance encounter at a party. When she asked, "How's it going?" B.J. gave a dismal account, saying that Scott's behavior had been hurting his reading progress. As a result, Scott's mom became upset (she hadn't been told about Scott's behavior problems), Scott became upset (he lost trust in his tutor), and the coordinator of the remediation program became upset (she'd been planning a parent conference, but was caught off-guard before she could contact Scott's family). B.J. had good intentions, but the coordinator of the reading remediation program was responsible for parent contact, and she should have cleared any communication with the parent. Of course B.J. was placed in an awkward position, and he was honest about his perceptions. In these cases, it's best to be cautious. B.J. could have followed his program guidelines and suggested setting up a better time and place to talk about Scott's progress—with the tutor coordinator.

When and where should information be shared?
Ask your tutor coordinator about the preferred time and place to have conferences with key stakeholders. When you discuss your student's progress, try to make sure you have enough time and privacy. Giving updates and reports in hallways, at student pick-up time in the parking lot, or in a faculty or staff lounge is unfair to your student and to you. Avoid the trap that B.J. fell into—don't provide informal news flashes about problems or concerns.

How should information be presented? You can provide key stakeholders with information about your student in positive and productive ways. This is particularly important when dealing with parents. Parents are usually deeply concerned about their child's progress in reading and writing, and they may be very emotional about the issue.

One way to structure your feedback is by using the TACT strategy described in Chapter 10 (page 117). This gives a framework for communicating with parents and others constructively and effectively.

We hear again and again that it takes a village to raise a child. Collaborating with the people who have a genuine interest and investment in a student is a vital part of your role as a tutor. Clear and respectful communication will help you and, most significantly, your student.

YOUR RIGHTS AS A READING TUTOR

Along with your responsibilities a tutor, you are also entitled to some basic rights. This is true whether you are a volunteer, a service-learning student, or a paid tutor. However, you'll find that these rights are tempered by some realities, and you'll probably have to be assertive to get your needs met.

The Tutor's Rights

1. *You have the right to receive training as a tutor, although you may have to initiate the learning on your own.*

2. *You have the right to a conducive tutoring environment, although you may have to use your own creativity to make it happen.*

3. *You have the right to the appropriate equipment and materials for tutoring your student, although you may need to be assertive to get these materials.*

4. *You have the right to receive help with troubleshooting and handling sticky situations, although you may need to find information yourself.*

5. *You have the right to be recognized for your contribution, although you may need to create your own rewards.*

1. You have the right to receive training as a tutor, although you may have to initiate the learning on your own.

As a reading tutor, you ought to receive training, particularly if you haven't had professional preparation as an educator. The reality, however, is that not all programs provide training. Be prepared to take charge of your own learning.

Think of your experience as a reading tutor as a learning adventure—an opportunity to learn from a variety of resources:

Learn from personnel at your tutoring site. Attend all tutor training sessions, but remember that these are just the beginning. After you get started, you'll have lots of questions. Continue to seek information from others who have more experience—your tutor coordinator, teachers, and other personnel.

Learn from your student. Listen to your student's needs, concerns, likes, and dislikes. Even very young children know when they're learning—and when they're not.

Learn from other tutors. Talk with other tutors to share joys and challenges. One tutor coordinator invites her tutors to an informal chat session two mornings a month. During that time, tutors share tips with each other about what has worked for them and what hasn't. If your tutoring site doesn't offer opportunities like this, ask your tutor coordinator for suggestions on networking with other tutors.

Learn from community resources. Become an active member of the literacy community. Attend book fairs, local reading association meetings, and tutor training sessions. You can also use the Internet to link up with your local community and with a larger literacy community. (See pages 10–11 for organizations that can link you to local resources.)

Learn from print and electronic resources. In this book, you'll read about valuable tutoring techniques that are compatible with most programs. You'll also discover additional print resources and helpful Web sites listed throughout.

Check It Out

Read with Me: A Guide for Student Volunteers Starting Early Childhood Literacy Programs by Chandler Arnold (Washington, DC: U.S. Department of Education, 1997). This brief guide to getting started as a literacy tutor was written specifically for college students. It provides information and resources on where and how to get involved.

The Reading Team: A Handbook for Volunteer Tutors K–3 by Lesley Mandel Morrow and Barbara J. Walker (Newark, DE: International Reading Association, 1997). This booklet provides an overview of tutoring basics and guidelines for planning tutoring sessions.

School Power: Strategies for Succeeding in School by Jeanne Shay Schumm and Marguerite C. Radencich (Minneapolis, MN:

Free Spirit Publishing, 1992). This book offers a collection of reading and study strategies for students in middle school and high school.

The Volunteer Tutor's Toolbox edited by Beth Ann Herrmann (Newark, DE: International Reading Association, 1994). This book is a collection of strategies and activities for helping students with reading and writing. It includes a chapter on how to help students with homework assignments.

---

2. You have the right to a conducive tutoring environment, although you may have to use your own creativity to make it happen.

Many tutors dream of facilities like this America Reads site: A large room in the school media center has been arranged into individual study carrels for tutor-student pairs. Books, writing materials, and other tutoring tools are readily available. The room is quiet and welcoming and communicates clearly, "This is a place to learn."

At most sites, however, space is at a premium. Tutors sometimes work in the back of classrooms, in cafeterias, in hallways, and at picnic tables on playgrounds. In such cases, tutors have to use their imagination to create an atmosphere for learning.

Edith Lemp volunteered in a fifth-grade classroom. School policy didn't permit her to take students from the classroom; she had to tutor in a room with thirty-two other children, the teacher, and an aide. The noise level was tolerable, but her student, Kent, a child with severe attention problems, was constantly distracted by the activity in the room. So Edith got permission from the teacher to set up a temporary tutoring center in the classroom. She put two student desks together and then used a cardboard display board from a school supply store to create a study carrel. Edith and Kent had some privacy, and the activity of the classroom was blocked from Kent's view.

Drew Allred tutored reading at a youth center as part of an after-school program. The only space for his one-to-one sessions with Tate was on a picnic bench in a hallway. Drew put all of the equipment and materials he needed for tutoring in a plastic container, which he and Tate referred to as the "portable classroom." The container included the following items:

- pencils, pens, and markers
- notebooks and paper
- scissors, glue, and tape
- books to read
- a list of "Books We've Read Together" (see page 65 for a blank form)
- their tutoring logs
- stickers and stamps for rewards

Shirley Kerns was a volunteer at a public school. Because the school was so tight on space, she tutored in any available nook or cranny. Rather than get frustrated, she took action. She asked the principal if she could use the stage in the auditorium for tutoring and got local businesses to donate equipment and materials. She developed a system and schedule for clearing the stage for assemblies and other special events. Shirley took the time and energy (with the permission of the administration) to create a conducive learning environment. The space still isn't ideal, but Shirley and her students agree that it's much better than what they had before.

Space is important, but it shouldn't make or break your tutoring sessions. Be creative and focus on your activities with your student.

3. You have the right to the appropriate equipment and materials for tutoring your student, although you may need to be assertive to get these materials.

Schools and nonprofit organizations are often short on funding for materials. Sometimes tutors have a hard time getting what they need. Teachers, who are used to being resourceful, can be strong allies. As one teacher put it: "I ask for what I need, and the worst thing someone can say to me is no. Then I just keep asking until I get a yes." You can put this idea to work for you.

If you need equipment and materials (particularly reading materials), talk with your tutor coordinator. Your best resource for reading materials is often your local public library. It's amazing what you can accomplish with the right reading material and some pencils and paper.

If you need additional resources, local service organizations (for example, Rotary International, Junior League, or Kiwanis Clubs), college fraternities and sororities, and religious institutions often make donations to literacy initiatives. Businesses can also be fertile resources for donations of money or other resources. It's worth asking.

4. You have the right to receive help with troubleshooting and handling sticky situations, although you may need to find information yourself.

As a tutor, you'll be able to handle most of the challenges of working with your student. And you have the right to get help with difficult situations—whether you're dealing with resource shortages, attitude or behavior problems, or students with severe learning difficulties. But you often have to take responsibility for getting information that will help you address the issues. Others can help if you ask for what you need, and keep asking.

Dara Powell, a college student volunteer, was paired with Derek, a fourth grader. At their first meeting, Derek let it be known that he did not want to be tutored and vociferously told Dara this using obscene language. Derek continued to talk this way during the next six weeks of tutoring. Dara didn't tell Derek's teacher or her tutor coordinator because she thought she should handle the situation on her own. Meanwhile, she became less and less enthusiastic about tutoring because of the stress.

Don't be afraid to ask for help and advice. You can't be expected to do what you haven't been trained to do. Chapter 10 offers additional suggestions for dealing with problems that may come up.

5. You have the right to be recognized for your contribution, although you may need to create your own rewards.

Helping someone learn to read and write is a reward in and of itself—and it's probably one of the main reasons people choose to tutor. Everyone, however, responds to a word of thanks, a note saying "good job," a token of appreciation, or a welcoming smile. Recognition reinforces the initial motivation and helps people see that their efforts are worthwhile. Just as the students you tutor need encouragement, so do you. Many programs formally recognize tutors for their contributions at luncheons or award ceremonies. Some teachers or tutor coordinators remember and acknowledge the tutors who help them. Students often express gratitude with notes, pictures, or letters.

Although you have a right to rewards and recognition, they may not come from the institution, the tutor coordinator, or your student. You'll probably need to create your own internal rewards. Some days will go better than others, but focus on the joys of tutoring. At the end of each tutoring session, thank your student for something he or she did that helped you grow as a tutor. Before you leave the tutoring site, thank the site supervisor for what you are learning from the experience. As you travel home, think about one good thing that happened during the tutoring session—and dwell on it. Focus on the positive, and you'll be rewarded.

READY, SET, GO!

Once you commit to a program and understand your general rights and responsibilities as a reading tutor, you're ready to begin. Before your first tutoring session, spend some time becoming familiar with your tutoring site. Many programs offer an orientation for new tutors; some don't. Although you probably asked many questions when you were deciding whether the program was right for you, you'll likely have more once you've made the commitment.

If your tutoring program doesn't have a formal orientation, make an appointment to meet with the person responsible for coordinating the program. At a school, the tutor coordinator might be a principal, assistant principal, school secretary, reading specialist, classroom teacher, or school psychologist. At other institutions, he or she might be a program director, secretary, or volunteer. Chances are, the tutor coordinator is a busy person who wears many other hats. If you just drop in, he or she may not have time to answer your questions or will provide scattered information on the run. It's best to make an appointment first.

To guide your conversation, use the Tutoring Site Orientation Questionnaire on pages 21–23. Review the questionnaire before your appointment to identify any concerns you have that aren't covered there. Attach a list of additional questions that occur to you. Notice that questions 26–31 assume that certain procedures, policies, and publications (for example, a program calendar) already exist. Make sure that you come away from your meeting with an understanding of these policies and procedures, and with any publications you need.

Tutoring Site Orientation Questionnaire

1. Where is the tutoring site?

Organization _____

Address _____ Phone _____

_____ Fax _____

_____ Email _____

2. What type of literacy program is used at the site?

☐ literature-centered   ☐ professional-centered

☐ schoolwork-centered   ☐ tutor-centered

☐ materials-centered   ☐ combination

3. Who is my direct supervisor at the site?

Name _____ Phone _____

Job title/position _____ Email _____

4. Who are other key staff at the site?

Name _____ Phone _____

Name _____ Phone _____

Name _____ Phone _____

5. How should I address administrators and other personnel at the site?

_____

6. What is my term of service? (*Examples:* one semester; one year.)

Term _____ Start date _____ End date _____

7. What are the dates and times for my tutoring sessions?

_____   _____   _____

_____   _____   _____

continued →

Tutoring Site Orientation Questionnaire continued . . .

8. What are the dates and times for training sessions?

_____   _____   _____

_____   _____   _____

9. When is my trial period? _____

10. When are my reviews?

_____   _____   _____

11. How should I address my students? _____

12. How should my students address me? _____

13. What are the procedures for signing in at the site?_____

_____

14. What is the policy on wearing name tags?_____

15. What is the dress code? _____

16. How should I report when I am sick or plan to be on vacation? _____

_____

17. What is the policy for using the telephone at the site to make personal calls? _____

_____

18. Where are the bathrooms for my student and me? _____

_____

19. What are the procedures for taking my student to and from tutoring sessions?_____

_____

continued ⟶

Tutoring Site Orientation Questionnaire continued . . .

20. Where will I find the equipment and materials available to me?_____

_____

21. How should I request or purchase additional equipment and materials if and when they are

needed? _____

22. What are the procedures for communicating with key stakeholders (parents, teachers, etc.)?

_____

_____

23. What procedures should I follow to plan tutoring sessions? _____

_____

_____

24. How should I record my student's progress? _____

_____

25. How will I be evaluated as a tutor?_____

_____

26. Do I have a copy of the program calendar?   ☐ Yes   ☐ No

27. Do I know when the site is closed for holidays?   ☐ Yes   ☐ No

28. Do I have a copy of the site handbook (if available)?   ☐ Yes   ☐ No

29. Am I familiar with the policies on tutor liability?   ☐ Yes   ☐ No

30. Am I familiar with procedures for reporting child abuse or neglect?   ☐ Yes   ☐ No

31. Do I know the procedures for fire drills, student illness,   ☐ Yes   ☐ No
and other emergencies?

Please help me learn to read. I'm just tired of being dumb.
—Fourth-Grade Student with LD

CHAPTER 3

CHALLENGES IN LEARNING TO READ AND WRITE

Virginia Keel, a retired banker, was looking for something different to do when she decided to volunteer as a reading tutor in an elementary school near her home. She'd read in the local newspaper that the school had some of the lowest achievement test scores in the state. As the principal explained when Virginia went in for orientation, over 90 percent of the school's students received free or reduced-price lunches, and the problems of poverty had a profound effect on many students and their families. The school, both its staff and students, needed help.

Virginia met with the fourth-grade students she'd been assigned to tutor: Jason could barely read his own name. Carlos could "read" many words but didn't know what they meant. Tamika could read
fairly well, but her spelling and writing were indecipherable. Virginia was amazed by the wide range of needs her students had.

Now, after tutoring for many years, Virginia offers advice to the new tutors she helps train: "My biggest misconception was that all students learn to read and write in the same way. I thought that if I had a 'reading Rosetta stone,' I could help all students quickly and easily, step by step. But there's no easy answer. It takes work, and the willingness to try new methods. Not everything works for every student. I've learned, though, that if I'm flexible and really attuned to my students, I can help them with their specific needs."

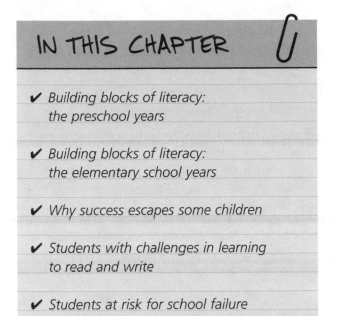

IN THIS CHAPTER

✔ *Building blocks of literacy: the preschool years*

✔ *Building blocks of literacy: the elementary school years*

✔ *Why success escapes some children*

✔ *Students with challenges in learning to read and write*

✔ *Students at risk for school failure*

As Virginia Keel learned, students have many challenges in learning to read and write for many different reasons. How a child learns to read and write is as individual as a fingerprint. People learn in individual ways based on their experiences, opportunities, learning styles, abilities, and interests.

In this chapter, you'll read about the building blocks of learning to read and write. There are reasons some children succeed in putting the blocks together and also reasons why success escapes some children. Some students are at risk of school failure for social and emotional reasons. Others have challenges in learning to read because of a disability. Some children have problems learning to read English because they are still learning the language. This chapter provides an overview of how children learn to read and write, and why some children have difficulties.

BUILDING BLOCKS OF LITERACY: THE PRESCHOOL YEARS

If you saw the movie *Three Men and a Baby,* you might remember a scene in which the character played by Tom Selleck reads aloud from a sports magazine to baby Mary—the topic is boxing. When a friend questions his reading material, Selleck's character says that it doesn't matter what you read, it's all in the tone of your voice. While some might not agree with his tactics, the character at least recognized the importance of reading to children, even during infancy.

Researchers, educators, and parents have begun to realize the importance of early literacy experiences. Kindergarten may be too late for some children—by then they may be far behind classmates who've had an early push from parents who read to them. Some kids have trouble catching up.

Preschool children are natural language magnets. Most know a great deal about the spoken language used in their homes and learn new words at a frantic pace. How many times have you heard parents exclaim: "I have to be so careful about what I say around my child. She picks up on everything—and sometimes that can be embarrassing!"

This knowledge of spoken language forms the basis for written language skills (reading and writing). But understanding speech is just the beginning. To learn to read and write, early readers also need other basic building blocks:

Book awareness—an understanding of what a book is and how it works. This includes recognizing the basic parts of a book (cover, title, pages, etc.), recognizing the front and back of a book, and understanding page turning.

Print awareness—an understanding of how our print language works. This includes not only being able to name and differentiate the letters of the alphabet, but also understanding other print conventions—seeing words and sentences, recognizing punctuation marks, knowing that print in English runs from left to right and from the top to the bottom of the page.

Phonological awareness—the ability to hear sounds in words and detect differences in those sounds. Some are pretty tricky for children and people learning a new language; for instance, the difference between *b* and *p*.

Environmental print awareness—the ability to read familiar signs and symbols. Stop signs, fast-food signs, and store signs are among the first things children learn to identify. For example, Jamie read her first word on a clothing tag while her mom was folding laundry. The word was *Venture*, the label of the discount store where the clothing was purchased.

Story awareness—an understanding of the basic structure of a story. This includes recognizing that stories have a beginning, middle, and end, and that they have characters and occur in a particular setting (time and place).

How do children acquire these building blocks? What makes a successful beginning reader and writer? Many factors are required:

Adult role models. Children learn about books, letters, words, and stories because they notice people reading and writing. If they see their special adults reading and writing, they want to learn to do these things, too. They are curious about letters and words and want to practice "writing" them.

Exposure to print. Children need to see the written word through a variety of media, whether books, magazines, newspapers, packages, or games. They also need exposure to writing materials: paper, pencils, markers, crayons, magnetic letters, or computer software.

A rich history of being read to. Reading aloud to children stimulates brain development. Children who have been read to since infancy have a head start not only in understanding books and print, but also in vocabulary and conceptual knowledge. The more words and concepts children recognize in spoken language, the easier reading comprehension becomes.

Encouragement to read and write. When someone in the child's home or preschool notices or encourages a child's budding interest in "reading" books and "writing" messages, the child is apt to continue and want to learn more.

BUILDING BLOCKS OF LITERACY: THE ELEMENTARY SCHOOL YEARS

Formal instruction in basic skills has traditionally been the backbone of the elementary curriculum (the three Rs: reading, 'riting, and 'rithmetic) beginning in first grade. During the elementary grades, students typically receive instruction in these building blocks of reading and writing:

Word recognition—the ability to read single words alone or in context. This includes being able to recognize very common words (such as *and, the, was*) on sight and to sound out new words.

Vocabulary—knowledge of word meanings. Students sometimes learn new vocabulary within the framework of a specific subject, such as science or social studies. They also learn new words when studying a work of literature. In some cases, teachers focus on general vocabulary development, asking students to learn lists of words that may or may not be related in some way.

Reading comprehension—the ability to understand the message of the writing. This includes understanding both the literal and implied meaning and being able to respond or react.

Handwriting—skill in both manuscript (printing) and cursive (script) writing. In some school districts, students also learn keyboarding and word processing as part of their writing curriculum.

Spelling—skill in writing words according to standard conventions. Early stages of spelling development include using *invented spellings,* or nonstandard spellings based on what children hear and remember about the visual representation of a word. For example, a first grader might invent *MTR* for mother. Spelling instruction includes teaching common spelling patterns (root words, prefixes, and suffixes) and "outlaws," or irregular words that are inconsistent with spelling patterns (*dough, there, buy*).

Grammar and composition—knowledge of language conventions (parts of speech, punctuation, mechanics) and writing in a variety of forms (short stories, essays, business and friendly letters, etc.). Grammar and composition may be taught separately or in tandem. Today's students typically learn about writing as a process—from brainstorming to editing to producing a polished piece of writing.

Reading and writing instruction varies considerably from district to district, school to school, and classroom to classroom. Some programs teach reading and writing as separate subjects. Others integrate the two skills. Some programs are guided by reading and writing textbooks. Other programs use children's literature (called *trade books*) and children's own writing rather than textbooks. Research has not identified one "best" or "right" way to teach reading and writing to all students. Good teachers can teach students to read using almost any kind of program. However, there are several essential aspects of any reading program:

Systematic instruction in reading and writing. We probably all have heard of someone who was "self-taught" in reading and writing. Very few people, however, learn to read and write without support and instruction. Instruction can be formal or more incidental; it can take on many different forms and represent many different models. But for most learners, instruction is imperative.

Ample time for students to practice their reading and writing to become more proficient and fluent. If you learned to drive using a stick shift, your driving was probably pretty clunky at first. Everything was new and awkward. None of the necessary steps (pushing down the clutch, shifting to the proper gear) were automatic. Your driving improved only through practice. It's the same with reading and writing. The more students read and write—the more they practice—the more fluent they become. After a while, they can concentrate less on the reading and spelling of individual words and more on getting the main ideas.

Opportunities for students to pursue personal interests in reading and writing. Youngsters who are avid readers have developed an interest in reading and writing, whether on their own or with the help of others. They have discovered genuine, engaging avenues to use these communication skills.

Assuring that readers and writers make progress toward success requires careful monitoring and assessment. It's important to recognize early on when students aren't making satisfactory progress and to react quickly. Students who have a history of difficulty with learning to read and write need even more intensive and regular checkups to keep them on track.

WHY SUCCESS ESCAPES SOME CHILDREN

Emma had two sons, Daniel (the older) and Max (two years younger). During their preschool and early elementary years, both boys did well in school. They were star pupils. Then, when Daniel was in third grade, something happened. His grades began to slip in every subject. Eventually he was evaluated, and Emma discovered he had a reading-related learning difficulty. Daniel's problems with reading continued throughout his academic career, while Max went on to soar at school.

Emma had trouble understanding Daniel's learning difference (LD). "I did all the right things," she said. "I sent them to preschool. I read to them. I took them to the library. I helped both boys with their homework. It was hard for me to see why one of my sons did so well in school and the other didn't. Daniel was obviously bright and worked hard, but reading remained very difficult for him."

Even when children have rich early learning opportunities, like Daniel did, mastering reading and writing can come slowly. Daniel was fine with the initial stages of reading, but as the demands got more rigorous, he couldn't keep up and needed new strategies to make progress.

There are many reasons why some students have difficulty in learning to read and write. In general, these reasons cluster in three categories: the student, society, and the school experience. As you'll note very quickly, the categories overlap.

The Student

Reading and writing are very complex tasks. These tasks can break down at any point and for many reasons. Some of the many individual factors that can cause breakdowns include differences in

- sensory functioning
- brain function
- motivation
- memory
- attention span
- language abilities
- intelligence
- self-esteem
- vocabulary
- prior knowledge

Students who have difficulty understanding the idea that written spellings represent spoken words will have trouble learning to read. Likewise, students who have trouble transferring their knowledge of spoken language to reading struggle with the written word. Children with limited proficiency in English and those with hearing or speech impairments will likely need extra help. Children who have a small vocabulary or little prior knowledge of the concepts they are reading about often have trouble with comprehension. Some children have many individual factors that affect their ability to learn to read.

Society

Children don't learn in a vacuum. Social and family conditions strongly affect the physical and mental well-being of youngsters. Learning to read and write is difficult if

- your basic needs (food, shelter, safety) are not being met

- you lack books and other literacy materials

- your parents have trouble with reading and writing, and you're beginning school with less reading experience and fewer skills than other students

- your home life is stressed because of poverty, divorce, or family mobility.

According to a 1994 Carnegie report on reading, most middle-class children have had a thousand hours of story time before entering first grade; most children in poverty have had only twenty-five.

Tutors, like teachers, have little control over family and social factors. What you can do, as a tutor, is communicate with your tutor coordinator and other key stakeholders. Contact appropriate agencies if you have concerns about abuse, neglect, or emotional distress. (Your tutoring site should have policies and procedures in place for doing this.) As a tutor, your role is to make the tutoring experience as rich and wonderful as possible, an oasis in your student's life. By being a reliable and supportive person, you'll make a difference.

The School Experience

It's no secret that many schools are overcrowded and understaffed. Some children don't learn to read and write because their schools lack the resources to provide the intensive, individual assessment and instruction they need. Even when teachers do refer students for special services, evaluation can take up to a year, and valuable learning time can be lost.

Thousands of professionals do their jobs as best they can under sometimes unreasonable circumstances. One teacher tells the story quite well: "I believe reading instruction should be individualized in terms of reading level, interests, and varying cognitive styles of learning for all students, period! The reality is, I don't have the time or the resources to meet all of my own very high standards as a teacher."

Your role as a tutor is to understand the reading program at your student's school, to coordinate your efforts as much as possible with professional educators at the school, and to provide support by supplementing the school's reading program. Tutors can do what teachers find it impossible to do in a very busy day—give students much needed personal attention.

Try This Exercise

Why does success in reading and writing escape some children? Take a moment right now to think about all you must be able to do just to read this chapter. You must be able to

- *understand what a book is and what a chapter is*
- *locate the front and back of the book*
- *know to start at the top of the page and end at the bottom*
- *know that print runs from left to right*
- *decode individual words*
- *understand the meaning of individual words*
- *comprehend each sentence and understand how it relates to the sentence before and after it*
- *pick up the meaning of each paragraph and keep the flow of meaning rolling as you work through the chapter*
- *think about the overall meaning of the chapter and its most important points*
- *reflect on the authors' message, decide what is useful for you to remember, and think about points where you agree and disagree*

Wow! You're doing all of this at once, and chances are, you're not even aware of all these components.

Scott was having trouble in reading. His teacher saw him squinting and rubbing his eyes as he tried to read, so she recommended that Scott have a vision test. As soon as Scott got glasses, his reading skills improved.

Michelle's mother, Tina, worked full time at the mall. Michelle's father had dropped out of their lives, and Tina had to focus on keeping the family afloat financially. She didn't have much time available for reading to Michelle and didn't read much herself. Michelle went to kindergarten not knowing the alphabet. In first grade, she was in a class with thirty-seven other children. She still had trouble with the sounds of letters and didn't get the individual help she needed. By third grade, Michelle had fallen into a cycle of failure and had lost her motivation to try to read. By fifth grade, her vocabulary and reading comprehension were so limited that science and social studies had become a mystery to her.

Some students are like Scott. Their reading difficulties have a simple underlying cause. Fortunately, Scott's teacher was very aware of each student's needs, and Scott's dilemma was resolved quickly. Many more students are like Michelle. They get off to a rough start, and their initial problem leads to a second, a third, a fourth. There are many reasons now why Michelle can't read.

As a tutor, you may or may not have access to student records. Some information about students is particularly sensitive and confidential. The Student Reading and Writing Profile on pages 36–37 can guide you in seeking information about a student's strengths, challenges, and reasons for those challenges. Make an appointment with your student's teacher or your tutor coordinator, and bring a copy of the profile to your meeting and get as many answers as you can. Be aware that some information about your student may be confidential and withheld from you by law. You may feel that you're working in a fog without that information, but focus instead on what you do know and where you can help.

As a tutor, you're not responsible for evaluating students' reading and writing problems. Trained psychologists, special educators, and reading specialists conduct these kinds of assessments. But because you work closely with a student, you may discover something important in diagnosing a problem. You can keep notes on your observations, but do be careful about who has access to your notes. Check with your tutor coordinator to identify the appropriate channels for sharing your observations.

STUDENTS WITH CHALLENGES IN LEARNING TO READ AND WRITE

Who are the students you are most likely to tutor? Students who are particularly vulnerable to difficulty with reading fall into three broad categories: students at risk for school failure, students who are learning English, and students with disabilities. You'll likely see overlap among these groups.

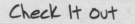

When you work with students who have special learning needs, you'll often encounter a veritable alphabet soup of abbreviations. Here are some of the more common ones you might run across:

ADD	Attention Deficit Disorder
ADHD	Attention Deficit/Hyperactivity Disorder
BD	Behaviorally Disturbed/Behavior Disorder
CD	Conduct Disorder
DD	Developmentally Delayed
EBD	Emotional/Behavioral Disorder
ED	Educationally Delayed
EH/ED	Emotionally Handicapped/Emotional Disturbance
ELL	English Language Learner
ESL	English as a Second Language
FAS	Fetal Alcohol Syndrome
HI	Hearing Impaired
IEP	Individualized Educational Plan/Program
LD	Learning Disabled
	Learning Difficulties
	Learning Differences
MR	Mentally Retarded
PI	Physically Impaired
SE	Substance Exposed
SLD	Specific Learning Disabilities
TBI	Traumatic Brain Injury
VE	Varying Exceptionalities
VI	Vision Impaired

For additional information, contact the following organizations:

Council for Exceptional Children (CEC)
1920 Association Dr.
Reston, VA 22091-1589
1-800-486-5773
http://www.cec.sped.org

CEC is an international, professional association of special education teachers, administrators, college faculty, and education consultants. Their principal purpose is to advance the education of all exceptional children and youth.

Hello Friend
Ennis William Cosby Foundation
P. O. Box 4061
Santa Monica, California 90411
http://www.hellofriend.org

Established to fulfill the goals and dreams of Ennis William Cosby, this foundation is dedicated to helping people with learning differences reach their full potential. The Web site contains a wealth of resources for students, teachers, and parents.

LD Online
e-mail: ldonline@weta.com
http://www.ldonline.org

LD Online provides an extensive network of national and local resources; art work and writings by children, parents, and other people with learning disabilities; discussion groups with parents and national experts; a bookstore; and more.

Students at Risk for School Failure

You've probably heard the term at risk before. It's used in many different ways, but here it refers to students who are at risk for school failure. It became part of our language as a result of the 1983 report by the National Commission on Excellence in Education, A Nation at Risk. Students at risk can be old or young. They can be native English speakers or students learning a new language. Success in school can be difficult for students from all walks of life, although the problems of poverty very often exacerbate those risks. For example, according to the 1996 National Assessment of Educational Progress, fourth graders in the nation's poorest schools lag three to four reading levels behind their more affluent counterparts.

Researchers have identified four groups of students at risk:*

Students in need of remediation. These students have fallen behind their same-age or same-grade peers and need special help to catch up.

Students who have problems with the three Rs. Students who have difficulty with basic skills (reading, writing, mathematics) will have difficulty succeeding in other school subjects. The three Rs form the foundation for learning, and school success depends on early mastery of these skills.

Students who repeat a grade. Students who spend another year in the same grade face many educational challenges. Because of increasing public outcry about "social promotion" (students being passed to the next grade with their classmates regardless of grades or performance), many states are tightening promotion policies. The number of students who repeat a grade is likely to increase.

Students who drop out of school. Students who leave high school before graduation have limited employment opportunities and low potential earning capacity.

Some educators resent the term *at risk*. They like to think of students "at promise." Other educators say there are no students who have failed to learn to write and read—just students we have failed to teach. As a tutor, you'll have clear, distinct goals for your student. These goals can bring students at risk closer to being at promise one small step at a time.

Students Who Are English Language Learners

Most classrooms in the United States, especially in urban areas, have students whose primary language is something other than English. The numbers of these students are growing at a phenomenal rate. The Office of Bilingual Education and Minority Language Affairs predicts that by the year 2000, as many as 3.4 million students who speak English as a second language will be enrolled in U.S. schools.

The variations among students who are learning English can be great. Some students have recently immigrated from other countries, while others may have been born in the United States. Some students are the first in their families to learn English, while others have parents who are fluent in many languages, including English. Some students understand and speak very little English, while others have studied the language in their native countries. Some know how to read and write in their native language; others do not. Some students are familiar with the Roman alphabet used in English writing; others first learned to read and write using another alphabet or another writing system altogether. Some students acquire conversational English very quickly; others take much more time.

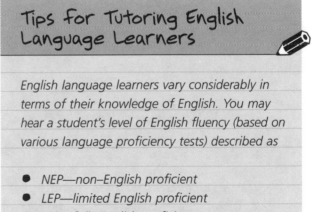

Tips for Tutoring English Language Learners

English language learners vary considerably in terms of their knowledge of English. You may hear a student's level of English fluency (based on various language proficiency tests) described as

- *NEP—non–English proficient*
- *LEP—limited English proficient*
- *FEP—fully English proficient*

The most important thing to recognize about students who are learning English is that they do not have a language *deficit*, but rather a language *difference*. Students who acquire English slowly may be very bright and have high potential for academic success. A tutor's role is to support students in their efforts to learn to communicate in English, to help them feel safe and comfortable in

---

*R.E. Slavin, N.L. Karweit, and N.A. Madden. *Effective Programs for Students at Risk.* (Boston: Allyn & Bacon, 1989).

taking risks with language, and to provide ample opportunity for practice.

Students with Disabilities

The most prevalent disabilities among students in the United States are learning disabilities (LD). You are more likely to tutor students with LD than students with other handicapping conditions. Students with LD have average or above-average intelligence, but they have some impairment in processing information and language. Under U.S. law, LD specifically does *not* include students who have learning problems that stem from a visual, hearing, or motor disability; mental retardation or emotional disturbance; or environmental, cultural, or economic disadvantage.

Students with LD may have difficulty in listening, speaking, reading, writing, spelling, or math. People with LD don't outgrow it; they have learning problems throughout their lives, and they need to develop appropriate strategies to cope with their difficulties. Many people prefer to use the term *learning differences* because it better describes what actually happens with these students. Students with LD *can* learn; they just need different strategies.

Myths About Students with Learning Disabilities

Myth #1—Students with LD are stupid. *Students with LD are typically bright. Some even qualify as gifted. By definition, people with LD have a significant discrepancy between their ability as measured by an IQ test and their school performance.*

Myth #2—Students with LD basically all have the same problems. *Students with LD are a mixed group of individuals with very distinct needs. Some have trouble with reading only, some have trouble with writing only, some have trouble with math only. Some have trouble with a range of academic areas. If you visit a special education classroom for students with LD, you'll quickly realize how different their needs are.*

Myth #3—Most students with LD have dyslexia and reverse letters and words while reading. *Some, but not all, students with LD have dyslexia (extreme difficulty with reading). Some, actually a very few, do have visual confusion involving letter and word configuration (vision-based dyslexia). Reversals, however, are usually a symptom of confusion, not a physiological problem. If anything, the majority of students with dyslexia have difficulty with phonological awareness, an understanding of the sounds of letters (language-based dyslexia). Lack of phonological awareness can create confusion about reading and causes thousands of youngsters to get off on the wrong foot when learning to read and spell.*

Some of the students you tutor may qualify for special education services. Students may receive part-time or full-time services in a special education classroom or in a general education classroom.

All students who receive special education services must have an Individualized Educational Plan (IEP). An IEP is a personal learning plan approved by the student's parents or caregivers as well as a committee of school personnel. You may not have access to your student's IEP because of confidentiality laws, but you may ask the student's teacher or parent about the educational goals on the IEP. The special education teacher, in particular, will be able to explain the student's learning problem and describe effective instructional approaches for that student.

When working with a student with a challenge in learning to read and write, you, too, have an opportunity to learn. Find out about the student you work with and think about the challenges he or she faces in learning to read and write. Talk to school personnel and your tutor coordinator to discover ways you can best help a student meet his or her individual needs. Turn to other resources and nonprofit organizations that may give you further information on effective strategies for understanding your student's difficulties in learning to read and write.

ABCDEFGHIJKLMNOPQRSTUVWXYZ

We cannot do everything at once, but we can do something at once.
— *Calvin Coolidge*

CHAPTER 4

PLANNING THE TUTORING EXPERIENCE

Ralph Morrison works at a large insurance corporation that has adopted a local school. The company provides books and supplies to the school, and employees visit the school once a month to read aloud to students.

Ralph was paired with Lamar, a second grader who was having a tough time with reading. At their first meeting, Ralph was astounded to find out that Lamar didn't know the letters of the alphabet. "I get mixed up about which one is which," Lamar said. Ralph was overwhelmed by how much Lamar didn't know. He was concerned that his coming in twice a month to read aloud wouldn't even make a dent in Lamar's progress. He wondered, Is it worth it?

Ralph talked about his concerns with the school's reading specialist, Lisa Carlisle. Lisa agreed;

Ralph couldn't solve Lamar's problems with reading and writing in the limited time they spent together. Ralph could, however, help Lamar make progress in specific areas. Lisa identified two goals for Ralph's time with Lamar: (1) work on book awareness, and (2) work on identifying letters of the alphabet, both in words and individually. She helped Ralph select interesting books to use to focus on those goals, and she showed him how to set up a regular routine for his sessions with Lamar.

"The time spent setting goals and developing an action plan saved me," Ralph said. "It helped me focus, and it also helped me feel that my contribution was worthwhile."

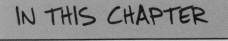

IN THIS CHAPTER

✔ *Understanding your student's strengths and challenges as a reader and writer*

✔ *Setting goals*

✔ *Documenting progress*

✔ *Setting routines*

✔ *What about rewards?*

Almost every self-improvement book and time-management guide begins with a simple premise: set goals and make a plan for meeting those goals. While a tutor's most important responsibility is to *be there*, regularly and on time, it's also very important to have goals you wish to reach with your student and to have long-term and short-term plans for meeting those goals.

Begin by gathering information. First, be sure you understand your role in the tutoring program. (See Chapters 1–2.) Second, learn about your student's strengths and challenges as a reader and writer so you know what your student needs help with. (See Chapter 3.) Only then can you begin to set realistic goals and document your progress toward success.

Once you have this information, the next step is to set up tutoring routines. You'll find guidelines for developing a pattern for your sessions and sample lesson plans in this chapter, as well as tips for motivating students through encouragement and rewards.

UNDERSTANDING YOUR STUDENT'S STRENGTHS AND CHALLENGES AS A READER AND WRITER

Learn as much as you can about your student. The more you know about your student, the better you'll be able to concentrate your efforts on areas where your student needs support. The Student Reading and Writing Profile on pages 36–37 is a tool for gathering this information. This profile will guide you in gathering basic information, such as your student's name, age, grade, and current reading level, as well as information on specific areas to work on, such as recognizing letters, reading comprehension, writing, and work habits.

Who can provide this information? As a tutor—volunteer or otherwise—you may not have access to some or all of the information that would help you help your student, because that information may be confidential. Start by asking your tutor coordinator about your student. He or she may know where your student has been struggling and be able to direct you to the information you need. Sometimes you'll need parental permission to find out more about your student, but parents are typically eager to cooperate in helping their child. The best sources of specific information are your student's teachers. It's imperative, however, that you follow procedures for getting confidential information about a student's test results and school performance. Specific information about your student should never be material for party or grocery-cart conversation. Even very young children are sensitive about their skills or struggles in reading. **Remember:** *Information about your student should remain confidential.*

Student Reading and Writing Profile

Student's name _____

Grade _____ Age _____ Current reading level _____

School _____

Teacher's name _____

School Reading Program

Title of reading textbook _____ Grade level _____

Other materials frequently used for reading:

_____

_____

Textbooks or other materials most frequently used for writing:

_____

_____

Student's Strengths and Challenges in Reading

	STRENGTH	CHALLENGE
Letter recognition	☐	☐
Phonological awareness	☐	☐
Word recognition	☐	☐
Fluency	☐	☐
Comprehension	☐	☐

Other reading strengths _____

Other reading challenges _____

Possible reasons for challenges _____

_____

_____

Student Reading and Writing Profile continued...

Student's Strengths and Challenges in Writing

	STRENGTH	CHALLENGE
Spelling	☐	☐
Handwriting	☐	☐
Comprehension	☐	☐

Other writing strengths _____

Other writing challenges _____

Possible reasons for challenges _____

_____

_____

Other Strengths and Challenges

	STRENGTH	CHALLENGE
Concentration	☐	☐
Memory	☐	☐
Risk taking	☐	☐
Confidence in reading ability	☐	☐
Confidence in writing ability	☐	☐
Work habits	☐	☐

Other strengths_____

_____

Other challenges _____

_____

Possible reasons for challenges _____

_____

_____

_____

_____

SETTING GOALS

Even once you have information about your role in the tutoring program, your student's program at school, and your student's strengths and challenges, chances are, you'll find that setting a few specific, *realistic* goals will be difficult, if not impossible, to do on your own. Moreover, if you try to set goals in isolation, you won't be able to take advantage of many of the resources available. Goals are most effective when everyone affected helps develop them.

Work with your tutor coordinator to set goals. Parents, too, should be involved as much as possible. At the very least, they need to be aware of the goals that are set and their child's progress toward meeting those goals. Students—especially older students—should also have a role in defining their goals. Setting mutual goals will help you meld your partnership, and when everyone has a stake in the outcome, meeting those goals will be especially satisfying.

The Goals for Tutoring Sessions form on page 39 provides space for recording the goals you set. Use the information you've gathered about your student and from other key stakeholders to guide you. Some of your goals should include what your student wants to achieve in the long term (for example, your student will be able to recognize and write all the letters of the alphabet, or your student will improve from a first- to a second-grade reading level). Once you've established reasonable long-term goals, you can plan the short-term steps that will help your student achieve them. For example, a short-term goal for a lesson might be to review two letters previously learned and to introduce a new letter using both reading and writing activities. Or perhaps your student will read a familiar book several times to develop fluency. Whatever goals you set, share them with your student, your tutor coordinator, and your student's parents.

DOCUMENTING PROGRESS

If you've gone through the thought and effort to set reasonable goals, you'll recognize the importance of documenting your student's progress toward meeting them. Some tutoring programs have systematic procedures for tutors to keep records of each lesson and document student progress. This can be the kind of paperwork that many people find tedious, but without documentation, tracking student progress is difficult, if not impossible.

If the literacy program at your tutoring site has a record-keeping system, plan enough time in your schedule to use it regularly. If the program does not have a system, the Lesson Log on page 41 can be a useful tool for informal record keeping. It provides a handy checklist for tutors to mark what they worked on during the session, as well as guided prompts for jotting a quick note about the successes and challenges of the session. It takes only a few minutes to complete. Some tutors fill out logs with their students as informal evaluations at the end of each session. You'll find a completed sample log on page 40.

Most tutors ultimately find the record keeping worth the time. As one tutor said, "After I leave the school, my mind is back on my own life. I might have a big exam, chapters to read, or research papers to write. Frankly, I leave tutoring behind. Taking two minutes to fill out the log helps me remember what we did. It also reminds me of things that really went well; I like to remember the good times."

Goals for Tutoring Sessions

Target date

Primary goal _____ _____

_____

_____

_____

_____

Secondary goals _____ _____

_____ _____

_____ _____

_____ _____

_____ _____

_____ _____

_____ _____

_____ _____

_____ _____

_____ _____

_____ _____

_____ _____

_____ _____

_____ _____

_____ _____

_____ _____

Sample Lesson Log

Date ___4/24___ Student's name ___Barkuni___

Today's goal ___Read and enjoy a book together___

Today we worked on

- ☒ Reading aloud
- ☐ Alphabet activities
- ☐ Phonological awareness
- ☐ Word recognition
- ☐ Fluency
- ☒ Comprehension
- ☐ Spelling
- ☐ Handwriting
- ☐ Composition
- ☒ Other ___build vocabulary___

What successes did you achieve today? ___We took turns reading out loud to each other.___

Attitude ___Great — loved the book!___

Reading ___Barkuni did a good job of predicting what would happen next.___

Writing ___We wrote about the story in our journal.___

What were your challenges today? ___understanding unfamiliar words by looking at context and pictures___

What are your goals for next time? ___Read another book together___

Lesson Log

Date _____ Student's name _____

Today's goal _____

Today we worked on

- ☐ Reading aloud
- ☐ Alphabet activities
- ☐ Phonological awareness
- ☐ Word recognition
- ☐ Fluency
- ☐ Comprehension
- ☐ Spelling
- ☐ Handwriting
- ☐ Composition
- ☐ Other _____

What successes did you achieve today? _____

_____

Attitude _____

_____

Reading _____

_____

Writing _____

_____

What were your challenges today? _____

_____

What are your goals for next time? _____

_____

SETTING ROUTINES

Most children like routines; they like knowing what to expect. Routines form the scaffolding for your tutoring sessions. Of course, it's fine to vary the routine from time to time—spicing up a session with something new and different helps keep students interested. A basic set of routines, however, lets your student know what to expect and helps you streamline your planning and preparation.

General Tips for Lesson Planning

1. The younger the student, the shorter the lesson. For children in kindergarten and first grade, thirty minutes is long enough. For children in second and third grade, forty-five minutes is fine. For older students, one hour. You may want to start with a shorter time and then build up.

2. The younger the student, the shorter the individual activities within the lesson. Keep moving from activity to activity.

3. Include a clearly defined objective for each lesson. Know what you want to accomplish.

4. Make a list—mental or otherwise—of the materials and equipment you'll need.

5. Plan a sequence of activities for the lesson that includes regular routines:

- the greeting
- the agenda
- the work plan
- special activity or surprise
- wrap-up

A sample lesson plan is included on page 43, and you'll find a reproducible lesson planning form on page 44.

Tips for Tutoring English Language Learners

*If your student speaks very little English, and you speak very little of your student's native language, think **first things first**. Keep routines simple and predictable so your student will feel comfortable and more assured about what is going to happen. Work out routines to help your student develop a sense of safety and security, belonging, and self-esteem.*

Start by making sure your student feels safe and secure with you. A child who is new to the country and new to a school can be understandably confused when a stranger comes to work with him or her. Make sure someone has explained (in your student's own language) who you are and why you are here to help. Let your student know what to expect, and set routines for breaks and leaving and returning to the classroom.

Help your student develop a sense of belonging and acceptance. Spend time getting to know your student. The All About Me activity (see page 50) and the dialogue journals (see pages 52–57) are excellent tools for getting started. If possible, find a picture book related to your student's homeland. Use that as a discussion starter to learn more about your student, his or her family, and the culture.

Provide positive feedback frequently to encourage self-esteem. You want to provide an environment where your student feels comfortable taking risks and speaking in a language that isn't necessarily comfortable. Offer encouragement. Speak slowly and clearly, and model your own willingness to take risks in your student's native language. Focus on what your student knows and what he or she can communicate. When you identify areas that need improvement, focus on one at a time and provide encouragement when making corrections.

Sample Lesson Plan

Student's name ___Tessa___

Tutor's name ___Billy___

Today's goal ___Read and enjoy a book___

Materials

___book___

___drawing paper___

___crayons___

1. Greetings

2. Review agenda for the day

3. Work plan (regular activities in order) ___Read aloud I Meant to Clean My___
___Room Today, by Miriam Nerlove___

4. Special activity or surprise ___Make a cartoon of key events in the story___

5. Wrap-up
- ___Record book on our reading list___
- ___Rate the book___
- ___Choose book for the next time___

Lesson Planner

Student's name _____

Tutor's name _____

Today's goal _____

Materials

_____   _____

_____   _____

_____   _____

_____   _____

1. Greetings

2. Review agenda for the day

3. Work plan (regular activities in order) _____

_____

_____

_____

4. Special activity or surprise _____

_____

_____

_____

5. Wrap-up _____

_____

_____

The Greeting

Start each meeting by greeting your student warmly. Some people have a special greeting that they always like to use—for example, Ennis Cosby's favorite greeting "Hello, friend!" Or "What do you know that's good?" You may not have a trademark greeting, but meeting your student with a smile and a few kind words is the best way to start each session—even if your student was a "tutor's terror" the last time you met. Give your student (and yourself) a fresh start.

Use a few minutes of the session to touch base with your student. Learning about what's going on for your student in school and at home develops rapport and enriches your experience together. The more you know about each other, the better you'll be able to serve as a mentor or role model. This doesn't need to take long, and, as a matter of fact, it shouldn't. You have work to do together.

The Agenda

Try to remember the most hassle-free flight you've ever taken. Perhaps what made a long flight memorable was that the flight attendants provided an agenda. You were pleasantly informed when meals would be served, when movies would be shown, and what your general flight plan was. You knew what to expect, and the flight attendants probably saved themselves an hour of fielding questions.

Overviews (or, in educational terms, advance organizers) help because they let people know what to anticipate and how to identify the main points. Providing a brief overview of the agenda for the session can help you and your student know what to expect and feel more at ease.

The Work Plan

Develop a work plan that includes a regular sequence of activities based on your goals. This should be simple and direct. For example, if your goal for the day is to work on the letter B, your work plan could involve introducing the letter B to your student, then completing activities on that letter in your student's classroom activity book. Your work plan might change as your student meets the goals. Or if your student seems to be having difficulty meeting certain goals, you might need to evaluate and change your routine. For example, if the lessons in the activity book aren't working, you could try to provide other ways of helping your student learn the letter—by forming it in clay or sand, for example. Some students need to feel the shapes of the letters to learn and remember them.

Special Activity or Surprise

Routines provide structure, but they can also foster boredom. Use your imagination to spice up your regular routine with a special activity or surprise from time to time. For example, you might bring a special book to read aloud or plan a game that reinforces the lesson plan. To get your imagination rolling, take a look at Chapter 9, which provides tips to make your tutoring sessions lively and fun. Invite your student to come up with ideas for making your time together more fun.

Wrap-up

Spend a few minutes at the end of each session to summarize what you have covered and outline the next session:

- Reflect on what you and your student accomplished.
- Give praise and encouragement for what your student did well.
- Note the date of the next session.
- Set goals for the next session.

A wrap-up routine helps you and your student leave the session with positive thoughts and anticipation for next time. This is also a good time to let your student know if you'll be away or remind your student that holidays or vacations are approaching.

WHAT ABOUT REWARDS?

Sprinkling tutor sessions with genuine, specific words of encouragement should be a regular part of each lesson. Encouraging words nudge students to keep going. Your students will feel even more rewarded when they learn something that escaped them in the past.

But should you plan tangible rewards for your student in addition to these intrinsic rewards? Yes . . . and no. Here are some do's and don'ts to keep in mind:

Do give rewards that recognize specific behavior and achievements. In other words, let your student know why he or she is receiving the reward.

Do give rewards that are meaningful to your student. One tutor gave a University of Miami pencil to a student, and she refused it—she was a Florida State Seminoles fan.

Do be aware that students with behavior disorders or attention deficit disorder may be on a specific behavior management plan recommended by their special education teacher or psychologist. Abide by that plan whenever possible, using the same reward system.

Do be consistent about promises you have made about rewards. If you promised a sticker for every five new words a student learns, make sure you have enough stickers.

Don't give tangible rewards if this is against the policy of your tutoring program.

Don't give a reward if a student hasn't earned it.

Don't give food as a reward unless you clear it with the tutoring site first.

Don't show favoritism by giving rewards to some of the students you tutor and not others.

One of the most powerful rewards for students is being allowed to keep a book. Every time tutor Lisa Carollton's student, Jimmy, learned to read a book on his own, she gave him the book to take home. Jimmy was one of nine children of a single mother. Their family budget didn't include money for books, and his mother had precious little time to take Jimmy to the library. Until Lisa gave him a book, Jimmy had never had a book of his own. Jimmy kept every book he earned in a brown grocery bag, which he toted from home to school every day. He treasured his books, and he treasured Lisa.

Lisa paid for the books out of her own pocket and had the resources to do so. Other tutors may need to seek support in getting books for their students. Many local organizations distribute books as a community project. For example, the People of the Book project sponsored by Temple Beth Or in Kendall, Florida, raises money to give books to children in migrant camps and in schools in low-income areas.

*It's such a wonderful feeling to watch a child discover
that reading is a marvelous adventure rather than a chore.*
—Zilpha Keatley Snyder

CHAPTER 5

THE FIRST MEETING WITH YOUR NEW STUDENT

Juanita Bolden was one of the first volunteers to sign up when her church started a Saturday read-aloud program for neighborhood children. "I liked the focus on multicultural literature," said Juanita, "and I had loved books so much as a child myself that I wanted to spark the same interest in other young readers. I had this lofty vision of poring over books with an enchanted child and seeing that 'light' turn on when that child realized he or she could read.

"As much as I hated to admit it, I was chagrined when I was paired up with Robert. All I knew about Robert was that he was a terror—he always ran around the church making trouble, talked way too much and way too loud, and usually seemed totally out of control."

But Juanita determined to persevere. "At our first meeting, Robert and I talked about what we expected during our time together," she said. "We agreed we'd have just three rules: (1) sit at the table during reading, except at break time, (2) talk politely, and (3) work first and then play. I really had to remind him of these rules at the beginning, and although I had a hard time bringing myself to re-inforce those rules all the time, I found it was the only way to keep our sessions on track.

"I was amazed to find that, after only three weeks, Robert began to show real progress—not in reading so much at first, but simply in calming down, paying attention, and making an effort to follow directions. Robert and I developed a bond. We found we shared many interests, like fishing and vegetable gardening, and the books we selected and discussed brought us together. Now when I see Robert running around church, he's usually running up to me for a hug."

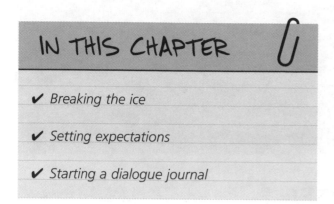

IN THIS CHAPTER

✔ *Breaking the ice*

✔ *Setting expectations*

✔ *Starting a dialogue journal*

The first meeting is your first chance to develop rapport with your student and set expectations for your time together. In fact, these should be your only goals for your first session. Spend this time getting to know each other and establishing routines and rules—that may be enough for your student, and you, without the pressure of an actual lesson. Because this session sets the tone for those that follow, planning it will make things go more smoothly.

BREAKING THE ICE

Before you and your student are introduced, make sure you know his or her name and how to pronounce it correctly. Greet your student with a friendly smile and handshake, calling him or her by name.

Your student may be just as eager as you to jump into reading, or he or she may be shy or apprehensive. Begin by putting your student at ease about the details of your sessions. Chat about the purpose and frequency of your visits in a way that lets your student know you're genuinely glad to be there. For example, you might say: "My name is Mr. Rosen. I'm going to be visiting you once a week—every Thursday about this time. When we meet, we'll read books together. That's why I'm here, to spend some time enjoying books with you. I've been looking forward to meeting with you, and I'm very excited!"

If your student is older, you might say: "My name is Ms. Butler. Your teacher has told me

you're making progress in many school subjects. She also told me about some areas where you need more practice. We thought that some one-to-one time might help. I'll be coming on Mondays and Wednesdays to work with you on your reading. I'm glad we're going to have this chance to work together."

At the beginning, focus on getting to know your student, and share something about yourself—your interests and why you want to help him or her. This can be an informal conversation, or you can use some tools to structure your information gathering.

- The Introductions sheet on page 49 can help you record basic information about your student. Knowing more about your student's family, for example, helps you get to know the student better. Ask questions, and write down your student's answers.

- Younger children and students just beginning to learn English can complete the All About Me sheet on page 50. It provides topics to prompt students to draw pictures. As your student draws, ask him or her to talk about the drawings.

- For older students (grades three and up), you can use the Getting to Know You Interview on page 51. You can ask questions and write down your student's answers, then turn the tables and have your student ask you the questions. The give-and-take is much more effective than having your student fill the form out on his or her own, and letting the student interview you creates an equal exchange of information. You can complete all of the questions during the first session or save some for later.

Introductions

Name _____

What do you like to be called? _____

Age _____ Birthday _____

Who do you live with? _____

    Parents' or guardians' names _____

    _____

    Brothers' names and ages _____

    _____

    _____

    Sisters' names and ages _____

    _____

    _____

    Other family members or friends _____

    _____

    Pets _____

    _____

Where do you go to school? _____

What's your teacher's name? _____

Where else have you gone to school? _____

All About Me

This is me!

This is my family!

These are my best friends!

This is my favorite animal!

This is my favorite TV show!

This is my favorite food!

Getting to Know You Interview

Name _____ Age _____ Date _____

1. My favorite TV show is _____

2. My favorite kind of music is _____

3. If I could get one person's autograph, I'd get one from _____

4. On the weekend I like to _____

5. My favorite sport is _____

6. I like to read about _____

7 My favorite magazine is _____

8. The best story I ever heard is _____

9. The best storyteller I know is _____

10. The person who does the best job reading me stories is _____

11. The best book I ever read was _____

12. In the evening I _____

13. I like to collect _____

14. I first got a library card when I was _____ years old.

15. I go to the library about _____ times a month.

16. I like to write stories about _____

17. I like to write letters to _____

18. My favorite subject in school is _____

19. My hardest subject in school is _____

20. My favorite person to talk with is _____

21. The most fun I ever had was _____

22. My favorite color is _____

23. My favorite food is _____

24. I wish I could go to _____

25. If I had three wishes, I'd wish for

    1. _____

    2. _____

    3. _____

SETTING EXPECTATIONS

Knowing about the purpose and frequency of your visits will help your student make the most of your time together. It's also helpful for you to set clear expectations about behavior during your sessions. Most experts in classroom management agree that it's important to do the following:

- Set a few clear rules.
- Talk about your expectations with your student.
- *Consistently* enforce the rules.

Children test limits, especially with adults who are new to them. That's one of their developmental tasks. So think about what's important to you regarding behavior during tutoring sessions, set some guidelines, and stick with them. Three to five will do; you don't want to overwhelm your student with restrictions, but you do need to set limits. Your expectations can be as simple as these:

- Be polite and use good manners.
- Listen to each other's ideas.
- Follow all school rules.

During the first meeting, talk with your student about each expectation and discuss examples. For instance, "being polite" means using words like *please* and *thank you.* "Listen to each other's ideas" includes being quiet while the other is speaking. "Follow all school rules" means that neither you nor the student can use words or tones of voice or actions that you wouldn't use in a classroom under a teacher's supervision.

Another way to approach this is to make "Tutor Rules" and "Student Rules." Doing so helps to establish a sense of partnership. The student is not the only one held to expectations; you as the tutor have responsibilities as well. These may be set up as follows:

As your tutor, I will

- Meet with you regularly.
- Bring the materials we need for our time together.

- Listen to your questions and ideas.
- Keep us on schedule so that we finish all our work.

As a student, I will

- Come to sessions ready to work.
- Be ready to talk about where I need some extra help.
- Listen to your questions and ideas.
- Follow the schedule so we can finish all our work.

The important thing to remember is that if you set rules, you must also enforce them. If you don't, you may as well throw your expectations out the window. Call attention to a rule when it is broken, and be prepared to impose consequences. Especially if you tutor at a school, you might want to follow your student's classroom rules. Check with your tutor coordinator for guidelines.

Consequences should be simple and not take up valuable tutoring time. Carry out any consequences right during that session; the next time you and your student meet, consider the slate wiped clean. Each student deserves a fresh start. You might even decide to reward students with a sticker or other small reward if they have no "reminders" at all during a session.

STARTING A DIALOGUE JOURNAL

One excellent way to get to know your student and build rapport is through a dialogue journal. A dialogue journal is a book that you and your student write together. In essence, it's a written conversation between you and your student, a journal that you share by writing to each other. As one tutor said: "Dialogue journals can be helpful, especially if you have more than one student. It gives kids a very real and personal use for writing that may motivate them to work harder in school or at least find a purpose for writing." Because the primary purpose of a dialogue journal is conversation rather than composition, students usually enjoy the process.

Dialogue journals have several purposes. They can help you

- model fluent writing for your student
- build rapport and learn more about your student
- observe your student's strengths and challenges in writing
- discuss books and other "assignments"
- evaluate your tutoring sessions, with your student's needs in mind

And they can help your students

- become more comfortable shifting from speech to writing to discuss stories
- practice writing with a purpose
- understand the practical use of writing

Dialogue journals can serve as the "bookends" for each lesson. At the end of each session, the student can write an entry in the journal, then you can write back. At the beginning of the next session, you can share the entries from the previous session.

Guidelines for Starting a Dialogue Journal

You can use a spiral notebook or something more elaborate as your dialogue journal. Pick one out together, or work with your student to dream up something exciting. How will you decorate the cover? The inside pages? With your student, write a list of the materials you'll need for your dialogue journal.

Model the first entry for your student, and be patient if early entries are brief. With your modeling, students will write more over time. And the more you write, the more your student will write. If your student has limited writing skills, let the student dictate the entry. Then read it aloud. Let your student predict or try to identify some of the words. Some students may be more comfortable drawing their part of the conversation at first, and you can encourage this, too.

Don't focus on spelling or grammar in your journal. Emphasize content, not form, because the ideas are what's important. If you notice a spelling or grammatical error in your student's writing, you can model the correct form in your own entries, but don't draw attention to it. In your responses to your student, look for something positive to comment on. Avoid sarcasm and negativity at all costs. The purpose of your responses is to motivate and to build rapport, not point out errors.

Tips for Tutoring English Language Learners

Dialogue journals are fantastic for students on a quest to become more fluent in a second language. Remind your students to focus on the message—not on form. The journal is a place to experiment. Dictation can be especially helpful in the beginning. Let your student dictate thoughts as you write them, and then you can respond in writing. Read what you wrote with your student. This can be a valuable record of your time together, and it will mark the student's progress over time as he or she becomes more fluent.

Keep the journal lively. Add artwork and photographs. You might even start the journal with a picture of you and your student together. Be sure to vary the kinds of writing that you do from time to time to keep things interesting. You can write stories for each other, describe a dream vacation, create a menu for a special meal, or anything else the two of you come up with.

As the tutor, take responsibility for keeping the dialogue journal and bring it to every session. If your student keeps it, it could get lost, along with the ideas and progress recorded inside. Then you'd need to start all over. At your final tutoring session, you can give the journal to the student as a keepsake. It's now part of your student's own reading and writing biography.

You and your student can also write about books you've read together. Some tutors like to retell stories they've read, others ask questions about the stories or the characters. You can reflect on the session—what went well, what needed work—or write about personal experiences. It's entirely up to you and your student.

Explain to your student that you are going to write a book together, and discuss the purpose for the book. Tell your student that the journal is a place for the two of you to talk about books, reading, writing, your session, and whatever's on your minds. Your student will write to you, and you'll write back. Educator Nanci Atwell suggests introducing the idea by saying, "Tell me what you thought and felt and why. Tell me what you liked and didn't like and why. Tell me what these books meant to you and said to you. Ask me questions or for help, and write back to me about my ideas, feelings, and questions." You may wish to add: "You can also write to me about your thoughts and feelings about the tutoring session. Let me know what you liked and didn't like. That will help me plan for the next session."

Here are some examples of dialogue journal entries:

Example #1: Ken and Damon

Ken became a tutor to learn to work with kids. Damon, a reluctant student with a spotty attendance record, was more interested in basketball. He talked about it as much as Ken was willing to listen. Ken and Damon decided to make their dialogue journal in the shape of a basketball. They used brown cardboard with holes punched in the side for the cover. They filled it with three-ring notebook paper trimmed to fit. From time to time, Ken brought in newspaper stories from the sports section and pasted them in the dialogue journal to ignite ideas for writing.

Ken and Damon wrote mainly about personal experiences—particularly sports—and they developed a strong bond. As Damon bloomed with Ken's tutoring, Damon's mother attributed her son's new positive attitude toward school to his experience with Ken, someone who cared.

Today I did something with a miami
huraches student. His name is Ked. He
is smart Just like me. We both like
basktball. We both like football to. Ken I want
you to know that I play football for the carol city
chiefs. I also play basktball for the carol city
chiefs to. I know that I started off wrong
but the little while your here I will behavie
if you want to work with me. Just tell Ms.
potter I will behavie I am makeing a comitr
come imet to you.

Love

Damon

Example #2: Vicki and Sandra

Vicki was an education student who became a tutor to discover the reality of the lives of children growing up in disadvantaged neighborhoods. Her goal was to be a great teacher.

Vicki purchased a photo album she and Sandra could use as a dialogue journal. On the first page, Sandra put a picture of herself and her elementary school. On the second page, Vicki added a picture of herself and her university. Vicki brought different stationery to each session to use for the dialogue journal entries so the pages were a kaleidoscope of colors and textures. Their journal included drawings and photographs as well as their writing.

Vicki and Sandra wrote not only about themselves, but also about the stories they read. In her entries, Vicki posed questions about the stories they read together, prompting Sandra's responses. Here are some samples:

Dear Sandra,
What books do you like to read?
Do you like Disney books and movies?
I do!
Love,
Vicki

Dear Vicki,
The Givieng Tree is my My favrite movies is Beauty and the Beast.
Good day.
Sandra

Dear Sandra,
Good day to you too! You picked two of my favorites: The Giving Tree and Beauty and the Beast. We'll talk about them next time. Maybe you could draw a picture of Belle next. visit. You are wonderful!
Love,
Vicki

Example #3: Jai and Twanda

Jai became a tutor because she wanted to fight illiteracy. An avid environmentalist as well, Jai often reused paper from the recycling bin at the computer center where she worked. All the pages inside Jai and Twanda's dialogue journal were printed with computer data on the flip side. Jai and Twanda made a cover out of construction paper. Jai's entries concentrated on getting to know Twanda better, making plans for future sessions, and promoting the value of literacy. Jai always signed off, "Well, till next time, happy reading!" Here's some of what Twanda wrote:

I love my family very much. I love my family by mom she helps me with things. And by my dad who buy me things or give me money. when at burdines. Last thing adout my brother who go place with me on specail times. Last but bnrt leat I told you about my famly who loves me very much and I love them very much too.

When you come lets go to the ibarary. I loke ot read authur books. I watch authur on tv.

Love,
Twanda

Different tutors emphasize different themes in their dialogue journals. These themes often reflect their reasons for becoming involved in the first place. Ken hoped to develop skills in working with children. Most of his comments were related to building rapport. Vicki, the education student, wanted to sharpen her teaching skills with students in a needy school. Her journal entries talked about the reading. Jai was anxious to make some contribution to solving the literacy problem. She consistently focused on the value of literacy in her entries.

In each case, adapting to the needs and wishes of students was the key to success. Ken encouraged Damon to draw pictures or cartoons when he was reluctant to write. Jai encouraged Twanda to write using invented spellings and nonstandard English. Vicki used a variety of techniques to keep her student motivated and engaged. Each took a different approach, but all used dialogue journals as a means to make their experiences with their students more meaningful.

CHAPTER 6

SHARED READING

Martha Fedor volunteered as a tutor twice a week at her son's school. One of the students she worked with was Patricia, a fourth grader who could barely read on a first-grade level.

Working with Patricia's teacher, Martha planned four steps for each session. First, Patricia read aloud a book she'd read with Martha during a previous lesson. This book was on a comfortable reading level for Patricia. Next, Martha and Patricia did what's called an "echo reading" of a new book—again, one on a comfortable reading level for Patricia. Martha read a sentence, and then Patricia read the next sentence. Third, Patricia read the new book a second time on

her own. Finally, Martha read aloud a book slightly above Patricia's reading level to model fluent reading and to get Patricia interested in other books.

Amazed with Patricia's progress over the school year, Martha observed: "Now I understand the power of reading aloud and repeated readings. The more Patricia read the same story, the more fluent and confident she got. She became more comfortable with trying to read new things. When my son, Clark, was little, he wanted me to read the same stories over and over again. Now I see how important that repetition was."

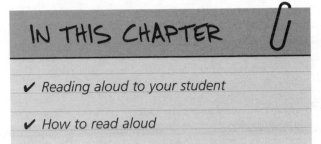

IN THIS CHAPTER

✔ *Reading aloud to your student*

✔ *How to read aloud*

✔ *Listening to your student read aloud*

✔ *Responding to your student's silent reading*

READING ALOUD TO YOUR STUDENT

Reading aloud to children is the best way to help them learn to read and learn to appreciate reading and writers. It helps them learn new vocabulary and grammar, and fosters a positive attitude toward reading. Research shows that reading aloud to students actually improves their reading ability. Even though parents and teachers are more inclined to read to younger students, older students benefit from being read to, as well.

Five Reasons to Read Aloud to Your Student

When you read out loud to your student, you

1. *model fluent reading*

2. *promote enjoyment and appreciation of literature*

3. *develop your student's knowledge of vocabulary and concepts*

4. *motivate independent reading*

5. *develop a bond between you and your student*

Choosing Books to Read Aloud

So many books! So little time! With the abundance of choices available, most people need some guidance to get started. Here are some guidelines to help you choose books to read aloud:

Start with stories *you* enjoy. If a book really appeals to you, you'll read with enthusiasm. You might select a book that was a favorite of yours when you were younger.

Keep your student's interests in mind. The Getting to Know You Interview on page 51 can help guide you in book selection. Knowing what television shows, movies, or activities your student likes can guide you toward a genre or subject area.

Choose books that make you react in some way. Books with basic themes like love, winning, courage, conflict, and fear prompt readers to respond in an emotional or intellectual way. Books like this are memorable to students and can help you generate discussion after your reading.

Choose books just beyond your student's reading level. You read aloud to your student in part to model fluent reading. You can choose books your student cannot read alone. Although you need to find books your student will enjoy, stretch beyond your student's reading level. Reading aloud offers a great opportunity to teach new vocabulary and concepts. You might also inspire your student to read the book when his or her reading level increases.

Choose books by a favorite author. When a student discovers a "magic book"—a real winner—chances are, he or she will enjoy other books by the same author. The same holds true for books with similar topics, themes, or genres. You'll also want to introduce variety, but for starters, find something that will "hook" your student, if you can.

Choose books on subjects your student is studying in school. Learning takes place when a student has both background knowledge and interest to bring to the study of a particular subject. By reading aloud a carefully selected story, you may be able to motivate interest and build knowledge of a current school topic.

Choose books that have predictable patterns of rhyme, rhythm, and plot. Younger readers love to anticipate the next words in a story that has rhyme and rhythm. They also like stories that let them predict what is coming next.

Bookstores and libraries abound with excellent books, and if the choices seem overwhelming, a librarian will be glad to make recommendations and point you toward appropriate books students enjoy.

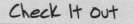

Check It Out

The following resources can also help in selecting read-aloud books:

American Library Association (ALA)
Resources for Parents and Kids
http://www.ala.org/parents/index.html

This Web guide offers links to lists of books recommended by age, as well as to award-winning books and Web sites for children.

Books to Build On by John Holdren and E.D. Hirsch Jr. (New York: Dell, 1996). Organized by areas of interest (history, language arts, etc.) as well as by grade level, each entry in this volume contains publication information and a brief summary of books appropriate for students K–6. E.D. Hirsch Jr. is also the author of *Cultural Literacy.*

Kids' Favorite Books: Children's Choices (Newark, DE: International Reading Association, 1991). This annotated list of books is compiled from the annual Children's Choices List, a joint project of the International Reading Association and the Children's Book Council. Individual annual book lists can be obtained by contacting

> International Reading Association
> 1-800-336-READ, ext. 266
> *http://www.ira.org*

The New Read-Aloud Handbook by Jim Trelease (New York: Penguin Books, 1995). One of the most popular resources on reading aloud, this book provides detailed suggestions for making the experience the best it can be, and it includes an annotated bibliography of books.

The New York Times Parent's Guide to the Best Books for Children edited by Eden Ross Lipson and Susan Luke (New York: Times Books, 1991). Instead of listing books by grade level, this book arranges them by degree of difficulty. The annotated bibliography lists everything from wordless books to books of interest for teens, and other indexes list books by subject matter to help match books to kids' interests.

150 Great Books: Synopses, Quizzes, and Tests for Independent Reading by Bonnie A. Helms (Portland, OR: J. Weston Walch, 1987). Geared toward readers in grade seven through adulthood, this book has synopses, quizzes, and tests. It includes books from many interest areas and classics. Each book is rated easy, medium, or difficult.

Teachers' Favorite Books for Kids (Newark, DE: International Reading Association, 1994). This annotated list of books for students in grades K–8 is a compilation of annual Teachers' Choices Lists (1989–1993) put together by the International Reading Association.

HOW TO READ ALOUD

Read-aloud sessions should be fun, and the following suggestions—which you can use before, during, and after reading—can help liven up your tutoring sessions. But don't let these ideas cramp your style. Use your imagination and creativity to come up with others. Most of all, just be natural.

Before Reading Aloud

- Choose three stories your student and you might enjoy.

- Read the stories before your session.

- Let your student choose which of the three stories you will read. Giving your student a choice is important, but limit choices to books that are appropriate.

- Relax.

- Set an atmosphere for enjoyment. Find a comfortable place to sit. Make sure the lighting is adequate for reading and looking at pictures. You both should have full view of the book.

Reading Aloud

- Read the title of the book aloud to your student.

- Read the names of the author and illustrator. It's important to teach your student that people write books (and he or she can write books, too).

■ Look at the cover and skim through the book quickly, noting pictures and other features of interest.

■ Ask questions to find out what your student already knows about the topic and thinks you're going to read about.

■ Read slowly, but don't talk down to your student.

■ Vary the volume and pitch of your voice to create a mood.

■ Act out parts of the story using voices, puppets, or props.

■ When using predictable books, turn the rhymes or patterns into games—let your student guess what word, rhyme, or phrase is coming next.

■ Encourage discussion and questions. Allow your student to interrupt you at any point along the way. That's what makes this time so special—your student can't do this when the teacher is reading aloud at school.

■ Share personal thoughts with each other about the pictures and story.

■ Offer additional information and explain key concepts and vocabulary when your student asks or when you think it's appropriate. But don't get bogged down in vocabulary; teaching two or three words per book is enough.

■ Use your sense of humor—laugh a lot!

After Reading Aloud

■ Ask your student questions about the story.

■ Encourage your student to ask you questions about the story. (Students love to do this and will try to trick you.) Model how to respond to questions. Feel free to say, "You know, I don't remember. Let's look back in the story and see if we can find the answer."

■ Let your student retell the story in his or her own words.

■ Relate the story to real-life experiences.

■ Share personal reactions with each other about likes and dislikes of the story and whether or not you would like to read another book by the same author.

Chapter 9 introduces tons of ideas for follow-up activities after reading aloud. (See page 111.)

LISTENING TO YOUR STUDENT READ ALOUD

Do you remember "round robin" reading, in which students take turns reading aloud from a story or textbook? Many people say they hated this classroom reading. They were so nervous about reading in front of a group that they didn't even pay attention to what anyone else was reading. One student remembered: "My teacher had us sitting in rows. Each student was supposed to read one paragraph. We went down the row and took our turn. I just counted ahead to see what my paragraph was going to be. I didn't listen to anyone else; I just practiced my paragraph."

Reading aloud can be traumatic. You probably don't want to have your student read aloud to you during your first or second session. Get comfortable with each other first. In the right situation, particularly in a supportive one-to-one tutoring environment, reading aloud can have many benefits.

Choosing Books for Your Student to Read Aloud

When you read aloud to your student, you can choose interesting books that are above your student's reading level. After all, you are the reader! When your student reads aloud to you, however, choosing books becomes a little more complex.

Student reading levels are usually reported as *grade level.* For example, we might say that a student

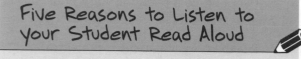

Five Reasons to Listen to Your Student Read Aloud

When you listen to your student read aloud, you can help your student

1. *improve word recognition*
2. *develop fluency through repeated readings*
3. *become more expressive and animated in oral reading*
4. *improve phrasing*
5. *develop confidence in oral reading*

is reading at a sixth-grade level. That means that a student can read material written for sixth graders in terms of sentence length and number of difficult words. We usually talk about the *reading level* of students and the *readability level* of books and other reading materials. Both are reported as grade levels.

When teachers talk about student reading levels in more depth, they frequently refer to three reading levels:

1. Independent level—the grade level of material students can read on their own. Students know all the words and can read smoothly and understand fully.

2. Instructional level—the grade level of material students can read with a little help from a teacher or tutor. Students know most of the words (missing one or two here and there) and understand most of the key ideas.

3. Frustration level—the grade level of material students cannot read. Even with help from a teacher, students cannot recognize most of the words and find understanding the key ideas very difficult.

In selecting books for your student to read aloud to you, stick to your student's *independent* reading level or *instructional* reading level. If you hit books at the *frustration* level, guess what? Your student—and you—will become frustrated.

Many books for children and young adults have a readability level code in the front of the book. It might look like this: RL = 4, IL = 6. That means the readability level of the book is fourth grade, and the interest level is sixth grade. For students who are older readers, you'll want to find high-interest, low-readability-level books (sometimes called *high/low* books). The trick is to keep students interested in and not insulted by the content.

You may be surprised to discover that your student can handle material that would otherwise be out of his or her reach—*if* the material is something of keen interest to your student or if the topic is one your student already knows a lot about.

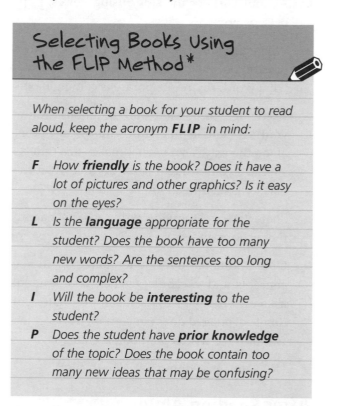

Selecting Books Using the FLIP Method*

*When selecting a book for your student to read aloud, keep the acronym **FLIP** in mind:*

F   *How **friendly** is the book? Does it have a lot of pictures and other graphics? Is it easy on the eyes?*

L   *Is the **language** appropriate for the student? Does the book have too many new words? Are the sentences too long and complex?*

I   *Will the book be **interesting** to the student?*

P   *Does the student have **prior knowledge** of the topic? Does the book contain too many new ideas that may be confusing?*

Another way to engage your student in reading is by selecting literature that represents your student's culture. This can help foster cultural pride. Sharing literature about your student's culture and your own (if it's different than your student's) can trigger powerful discussions about

---

*Jeanne S. Schumm and Charles T. Mangrum. "FLIP: A Framework for Content Area Reading." *Journal of Reading* 35 (1991): 120–124.

values, customs, foods, and holidays. Ask a librarian or your local bookseller to suggest appropriate books. Educators generally recommend avoiding multicultural books written before 1970; older books sometimes contain stereotypes in the text or illustrations that may offend or confuse students. In any case, preview the books you choose to prevent problems.

Tips for English Language Learners

If your students are learning English, **concept books***—books that focus on one concept such as colors, sizes, or numbers—are fantastic for shared reading. Concept books include appealing illustrations and photographs and are particularly good for developing vocabulary. You might want to select concept books related to what your student is studying in school, such as in science or social studies. Concept books are worth reading again and again.*

How to Help Your Student's Oral Reading

One of the most powerful ways to help your student become a more fluent reader is through repeated readings out loud. Reading the same passage or short book many times gives students the practice they need to become better readers.

Scan the story first. Find words that may be difficult for your student to read or understand. Go over these words before reading the story.

Allow your student to read through a story silently before reading it aloud. This is particularly important for students who are self-conscious about reading out loud.

Read a story, or part of a story, aloud to your student before asking him or her to read it. You can do this section by section, paragraph by paragraph, or, for less able readers, sentence by sentence. This frees the student from having to decode unknown words, clarifies the story structure, and makes reading more enjoyable.

Read the beginning of the story aloud to capture your student's interest. Then let your student finish the story independently.

Let your student record a favorite story on audiotape. You might want to work with your student to make a "greatest hits" cassette to give to parents. Your student might also want to record stories for younger children. (This is especially great for older students reading at a low level; it avoids the stigma of reading "baby books.")

Read "in character." If the story includes dialogue, assume the role of one or more characters and have your student take on another. Use different voices, accents, and inflections.

Keep interruptions to a minimum. Save phonics lessons for later so your student won't lose track of the story line or meaning. If he or she misreads several words, correct only those that affect the meaning of the story. (For example, it's more important to correct *can't* when read as *can* because the meaning changes. It's less important to correct *father* read as *daddy* because the meaning stays the same.) You might want to make a mental note of consistent errors to address at a later time.

From time to time you might want to record your student's progress in repeated readings using the Repeated Reading Progress form on page 64. You and your student can also keep track of the books that you read together using the form on page 65. Students enjoy seeing the number of books they've read grow steadily, and you can both enjoy playing book critic.

Repeated Reading Progress

Student's name _____

Book or passage read _____

_____

Rating Scale:

1 = great

2 = good

3 = needs more work

	1st reading	**2nd reading**	**3rd reading**
Word pronunciation	_____	_____	_____
Phrasing	_____	_____	_____
Attention to punctuation	_____	_____	_____
Expressiveness	_____	_____	_____

Comments: _____

_____

_____

_____

_____

_____

_____

_____

_____

Books We've Read Together

Student's name _____

Tutor's name _____

Rating Scale:

1 = We both liked it.

2 = One liked it; one did not like it.

3 = We both did not like it.

Title of Book	Author	Date Completed	Rating

RESPONDING TO YOUR STUDENT'S SILENT READING

Shared silent reading experiences are important—even when your student is on his or her own with word recognition and the basic mechanics of reading. Mature readers do far more silent reading than oral reading, but some students need support and encouragement to become comfortable with reading silently.

Five Reasons to Read Silently with Your Student

When you read silently with your student, you

1. *allow your student to skim, reread, or adjust his or her speed as necessary*

2. *give your student the opportunity to concentrate on meaning and devote less mental energy to pronunciation*

3. *model how to sustain concentration during silent reading*

4. *model how to respond to the author's writing in critical and creative ways*

5. *develop a bond with your student by listening to his or her reactions to what was read*

Choosing Books for Your Student to Read Silently

Students who are ready to read silently are also ready to learn how to select books. For some students, selecting books is difficult. It was really tough for Wayne, a fourth grader. He liked going to the school library with his class each week—not because he liked to pick out books, but because he

could hide behind the bookshelves and take some free time. Wayne got in the habit of avoiding book selection because he didn't know how. He never figured out how to find the "right book."

Book selection can be taught through direct attention to the task and with some patience. Take your student to the library he or she uses most often and help him or her become familiar with how books are organized on the shelves. Talk about different ways you choose a book—by topic, by author, by the kind of writing—and show your student how to find those kinds of books on the shelf.

Finding the Right Book

Here is a strategy you can teach your students for finding the right book:

- *Start with your interests. Do you like rock music, remote-controlled cars, hairstyling, rafting? There are plenty of books on all of these topics.*

- *No RIGHT BOOK yet? Move on to your needs. Do you need to learn how to play golf, redecorate your room, or research Colorado for your family vacation? You'll find dozens of books on these topics.*

- *No RIGHT BOOK yet? Think about your favorite movie or TV show. You'll find novels based on movies, biographies of stars, books about how TV shows and movies are made, and much more.*

- *Still no RIGHT BOOK? Talk to your friends, an adult you share interests with, and your friendly librarian. They will all have suggestions to pass on to you.*

Reading material for silent reading should be at your student's independent or instructional reading level. Teach your student to check the suitability of a book. Have your student read the first page silently, raising a finger each time he or she comes across an unknown word. If there are more than five unknown words on the first page, try to find a simpler book on a similar topic.

How to Respond to Your Student's Silent Reading

Students need to discover that they can read silently and that silent reading can be pleasurable. It's important that you read when your student reads. Modeling silent reading is *imperative*. If you're doing something else while your student is reading, you send the message that silent reading isn't really important. Start with brief silent reading sessions and then gradually increase the time.

Responding to your student's silent reading depends largely on the purpose for reading, whether it's for pleasure, for a class discussion, or for a test. It also depends on what's being read—fiction or nonfiction. Chapter 7 describes how to help your students respond to both.

A B C D E F G H I J K L M N O P Q R S T U V W X Y Z

> *We must not...ignore the small daily differences we can make which, over time, add up to big differences that we often cannot foresee.*
>
> **— Marian Wright Edelman**

CHAPTER 7

MEETING SPECIAL READING NEEDS

Krista Thomas, a twenty-four-year-old single mother, had been on welfare for three years when she connected with a federal welfare-to-work program. As part of the program, Krista was assigned to work at an elementary school as a reading tutor for children in first and second grade.

"Tutoring wasn't easy at first," Krista said. "Reading aloud to the children worked really well—it captured their attention and got them interested in books, but when it came their turn to read, some had a terrible time breaking down words and trying to pronounce them. I just wasn't sure what to do until their teacher showed me how to work with word patterns. Suddenly, I realized I could make a game out of this. My own kids have some favorite books that make a great use of word families

through rhymes, so I brought these in for the kids I tutored. Together, we could see—through simple words and silly, fun stories—how certain words really were like others. If you could read one, it was easy to figure out the rest. We made a game of predicting which word might come next in the rhyme—given the illustrations and other context—then sounding it out to see if our guess was right.

"Now I can't believe how much progress my students have made. I've got a knack for figuring out what kids like. I have a great time planning lessons and thinking of ways to make them fun. Tutoring has actually helped me, too. I've gotten better at taking risks. I'm going to work to become a paraprofessional, but someday, I'll be a teacher."

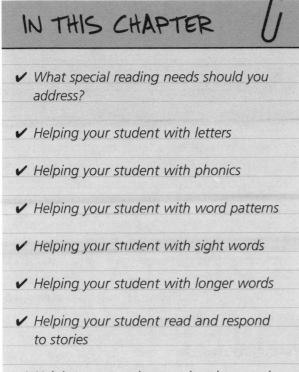

IN THIS CHAPTER

✔ What special reading needs should you address?

✔ Helping your student with letters

✔ Helping your student with phonics

✔ Helping your student with word patterns

✔ Helping your student with sight words

✔ Helping your student with longer words

✔ Helping your student read and respond to stories

✔ Helping your student read and respond to informational text

Just as students have many different reasons why learning to read is difficult, they also have many different special needs in overcoming their challenges to reading. Identifying your student's needs is only the first step. How should a tutor begin when a student needs instruction in everything from letter recognition to comprehending science and social studies textbooks?

While every school reading program is different, there are proven strategies tutors can use that will complement almost any instructional approach. This chapter will provide you with many ideas for approaching your student's specific problems.

Keep in mind that reading skills aren't necessarily related to age. Even though most students learn to recognize letters by the end of first grade, you may tutor a ten-year-old who still needs help with letters. Or you may tutor a seven-year-old who reads fluently but needs help understanding what she's read.

WHAT SPECIAL READING NEEDS SHOULD YOU ADDRESS?

For tutoring to be most successful, you should try to address the needs identified by your student's teacher or another professional. Likewise, the instruction you provide should complement the instruction your student gets at school.

Think about your own first-grade class. Do you remember what reading was like? If you went to school before the late 1980s, you were probably placed in a reading group. When the teacher met with your group—let's say it was called the Red Birds—you took turns reading from a textbook or *basal reader*, a book designed specifically for beginning readers. You might even have read "Dick and Jane" books, the most well-known example of a basal reading series. These books used simplistic stories with very short sentences and a tightly controlled vocabulary. Your teacher would help you with words you needed to learn and ask questions to see if you understood the story. While your teacher met with other reading groups, you might have been assigned seat work to do—usually filling out workbook pages. You probably had instruction in writing skills (handwriting, spelling, grammar, composition) at other times during the school day.

Around 1990, some schools eliminated basal readers altogether and began teaching reading using children's books (regular library books or *trade books*) instead. Many educators feel that trade books offer children more genuine reading and language experiences and help students cultivate lifelong reading habits. Also, the language in trade books is more appealing and natural than in traditional basal readers, even if some of the vocabulary is more difficult.

Today, most reading programs combine elements of both basal readers and trade books. Basal readers have changed since the days of Dick and Jane. The characters in reading textbooks today better represent diverse cultures, and basal reading programs now include classroom activities that emphasize the connections between reading and writing and spoken language. Many textbooks for beginning readers even include trade books within their pages. Most learning activities are far more stimulating than filling out workbook pages.

Regardless of the instructional materials used in the classroom, students are no longer necessarily grouped according to ability for reading. Some schools still use such traditional reading groups, but others have whole class instruction, and still others use more flexible grouping practices—some days small groups, some days pairing, some days whole class—depending on student needs and the skill or strategy being taught.

Because of this wide range of differences in how reading is taught, it's important for you to investigate what type of instruction is being used at your student's school. If you tutor at a school, you're in luck. Ask the tutor coordinator who you can talk with to learn about the school's program. The tutor coordinator, a reading specialist, a special education teacher, or a classroom teacher may be able to help you.

If you tutor somewhere other than a school, getting this information may be trickier. Check with your tutor coordinator first. He or she may be familiar with instruction in the student's school. If not, ask about procedures for contacting the school. The tutor coordinator may prefer to make contact with the school or may recommend that your student's parent get involved.

The questions on the Student Reading and Writing Profile (see pages 36–37) can help guide your conversation with school personnel to learn about the school's reading program and your student's particular needs. When school staff understand that you want to support what they are already doing, you should be able to find information about the instruction your student receives in school, as well as suggestions about how you can help.

HELPING YOUR STUDENT WITH LETTERS

When children first learn to read, they typically learn a few words by sight. They might learn to read their name, some words that are important to them (*mom, ice cream*), and words they see around them (*STOP, Kmart*). Many children learn to read whole words before they can recognize and identify all the letters of the alphabet.

Recognizing words by sight without knowing the letters of the alphabet has its limitations, however. Our writing system is based on an alphabet, so eventually students need to master the basic "ingredients" of our writing system—letters—to become mature readers.

What to Teach

Most experts in early reading and writing agree that teaching one alphabet letter per week (sequentially from A to Z) is less effective than teaching letters that are personally meaningful to the student. Typically, it's best to start with the letters in your student's first and last names. Then teach a few new letters at a time and review letters your student has already learned.

To determine what letters your student needs to learn, print the letters of the alphabet on separate index cards. Make one set of uppercase letters and one set of lowercase letters. Mix up the index cards and have your student identify the letters. Put the letters your student knows in one stack and the letters your student needs to learn in another stack. Then concentrate on teaching the new letters and reviewing the familiar ones.

Teaching Letters

Students need to learn some basic concepts about letters:

- *Letters have names.*
- *Letters represent sounds.*
- *Letters can have different shapes (capital, lowercase, manuscript, cursive) but still have the same name and sound.*
- *Letters make words.*

How to Teach Letters

Learning to recognize letters is easier when letters are taught in context. Teaching letters by themselves isn't effective with most students, especially students with challenges in this area. When you introduce a letter, talk about its shape and sound. Find a book that has many examples of the letter. For example, *The Berenstain Bears and Too Much Birthday* by Jan and Stan Berenstain (New York: Random House, 1986) is great for introducing the letter *B*. As you read aloud to your student, ask him or her to locate the letter. If you have been working on the letter *B*, ask, "Can you find a *B* on this page?"

When you teach letters, remember to connect reading and writing. Help your student form letters using the same writing style as your student's teacher. The handwriting charts on pages 130 and 132 can also serve as models for you. Supply crayons, markers, and other writing materials to add variety.

Some students require three-dimensional forms of letters to be able to learn and remember them. Magnetic letters or letters cut from sandpaper enable students to not only visualize but also feel the shape of each letter.

Here are some other ideas for teaching letters:

Find lots of alphabet books in the library. Read them over and over again to your student. You might be surprised by the number of ABC books available today. Make a game of it—take your student to the library and see how many different books you can find.

Write an alphabet book with your student. After you've read several alphabet books, you and your student can write your own. Perhaps your student can think of a favorite word to put on each page, or you could create an ABC book based on a theme, such as animals or food.

Make a dictionary with your student. Write one letter at the top of each page, and collect words to put in your dictionary. Add at least one word each time you meet. You can even illustrate the words and make it a "pictionary."

Develop letter radar. Be on alert for letters all around you—on posters, street signs, advertisements. Make a game of it—see how many *M*s you can find when you look around.

Find creative ways to introduce letters. You don't have to practice letters using paper and traditional writing utensils. Here are some fun ways others have tried:

- Bring in a large cake pan and a bag of fine sand. Pour the sand in the pan and show your student how to trace letters in it. Save the sand for future sessions.

- Younger children like to use finger paint to practice their letters. (This can be messy, so be prepared.) You can also use chocolate pudding instead of finger paint as a special treat.

- Another alternative to paper and pencil is clay. Have students form letters from clay or use letter-shaped cookie cutters to make letters.

Children's books and letters in the everyday environment are the best resources for teaching students about letters. The more "real" the materials, the better. Workbooks just don't motivate most students.

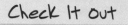

Check It Out

A Is Amazing: The Ultimate Alphabet Resource Book by Dayle M. Timmons (Carthage, IL: Fearon Teacher Aids, 1991). In addition to listing children's books for teaching each letter, the author also includes games, activities, and foods for each letter.

Alphabet Antics: Hundreds of Activities to Challenge and Enrich Letter Learners of All Ages by Ken Vinton, M.A. (Minneapolis: Free Spirit Publishing, 1996). Twenty-six chapters spotlight the letters of the alphabet from A to Z, celebrating each letter with quotes, fun facts, project ideas, vocabulary words, and more. This is a great resource for tutoring older students as well.

HELPING YOUR STUDENT WITH PHONICS

Phonics refers to the relationships between sounds and letters. As you've probably heard, phonics instruction can be controversial. Some parents and educators insist it's the key to learning how to read. Others believe the focus should be on immersing young readers in genuine, meaningful reading of children's books instead. They believe that teaching phonics and word recognition should be more incidental and based on individual needs.

What people *do* agree on is that letters represent sounds, and we have to know how letters and sounds relate in order to read words. Research shows that many students seem to learn this naturally and independently. Others need direct instruction and guided practice daily for several months, and some require intensive help.

The real debate over phonics revolves around not *whether* phonics should be taught but *how* it should be taught. Should phonics be taught directly, using carefully sequenced workbook pages? Or should phonics be taught more naturally, using children's literature and words in the everyday environment? Should phonics be taught through activities such as singing or using materials that enable children to touch and feel the letters?

Many of the students you'll be working with—students who are having difficulty with reading and writing—need some extra practice understanding the relationships between letters and sounds.

Tips for Tutoring English Language Learners

Experts debate the wisdom of teaching phonics to English language learners. Those who resist phonics instruction maintain that teaching sounds in isolation can be difficult—especially when the sounds are unfamiliar (for example, the sound of /sh/ for native speakers of Spanish). Also, phonics is often taught without putting words in a meaningful context.

All students need to learn to break the alphabet code, but phonics instruction with English learners comes with two major cautions: First, be sensitive to the fact that some English sounds aren't familiar or comfortable to students who speak other languages at home. You'll need to provide a safe environment for students to take risks with language. Second, realize that sometimes students can readily "sound out" a word to pronounce it but have no idea what the word means. Comprehension is vital to reading, so be vigilant in checking that students understand the words they are "reading."

What to Teach

Effective phonics instruction is built on a strong foundation of *phonological awareness*, the understanding of speech sounds. Phonological awareness consists of at least four components:

- detecting beginning sounds, or *onset*
- detecting ending sounds, or *rhyme*
- detecting individual sounds in a whole word, or *segmentation*
- taking individual sounds and *blending* them into a word

Effective phonics instruction also includes teaching about the relationships between sounds and letters. You can provide clear and direct instruction in reading and spelling various letters and letter patterns. The Phonics Primer on page 73 presents the basic components of a sound-letter relationship curriculum.

A Phonics Primer

Consonants: *Twenty-one letters of the alphabet representing twenty-eight sounds. Phonics instruction includes lessons in consonants at the beginnings, middles, and ends of words.*

Vowels: *Every word has a vowel—a, e, i, o, u, and sometimes y or w. Phonics instruction includes lessons in both short and long vowel patterns.*

Consonant digraphs: *Two or three consonants next to each other that create a new sound (for example: ch in child, teacher, or touch).*

Consonant blends: *Two or three consonants next to each other that are blended but retain their original sound (for example: bl in blow, trouble, or bulb).*

Diphthongs: *Vowel combinations that create a complex sound (for example: oi in oil, ow in power, aw in claw).*

R-controlled vowels: *Vowels followed by the consonant r. The r causes a shift in the pronunciation of the vowel (for examples: ar in art or car).*

How to Teach Phonics

Phonics can be taught directly using commercially published materials and programs designed explicitly for phonics practice. It can also be taught indirectly using literature and a student's own writing. One effective way to teach phonics is by using the Word Pairs game (see page 89). This procedure combines phonological awareness with reading and spelling.

When introducing a new sound-letter relationship (see the Phonics Primer above) here's a series of steps you can use:

1. Introduce the sound-letter relationship using a word your student is familiar hearing (*chair*, for example). Say the word out loud. Ask your student to say the word out loud.

2. Show the word to your student and point out the new letter or pattern you are teaching. ("Notice that the *ch* in *lunch* sounds like this.")

3. Talk with your student about other examples of the letter or pattern. Write each word on an index card or chalk board (*chips, chalk, lunch*). Underline the target letter or pattern, or use a different color pen or crayon to write it.

4. Show how the letter or pattern contrasts with other letters or patterns. In other words, provide some nonexamples. ("How does the *c* sound when it isn't next to the *h*? What about words like *cat*, *carrot*, and *counter*?")

5. Write sentences using words that demonstrate the new letter or pattern. ("Chan chopped the cherry tree.")

You may have seen and heard enticing TV and radio ads for commercial phonics programs that promise quick and miraculous results. Be aware that educators have expressed several concerns about the claims these programs make. Figuring out words is a process that uses three systems of cues: (1) phonics, (2) meaning, and (3) grammar. Some children overuse one or more of these systems and underuse the others.

For example, look at the sentence "I bought a pair of boots at the shoe store." A child who reads *boats* for *boots* is paying attention to phonics, because he or she correctly reads the word's beginning and ending. The student is also attending to grammar, because the sentence requires a plural noun. However, the student is not attending to meaning, because you can't buy boats at a shoe store. Which cueing systems a particular child needs to work on can be determined through careful diagnosis by a reading specialist. Remember that there is no "right" way to help every child read.

Prepackaged phonics programs can also present other difficulties. The method and sequence of commercial programs may not match the instruction in your student's classroom. The pacing can be very rapid and may confuse children who have reading difficulties. There's also a danger that a program can be considered a substitute to such important instructional practices as reading aloud.

Finally, many of these programs focus on fluency rather than comprehension. Students may learn to "read" on their own, but they may not learn to understand the message in the writing. And understanding written messages is the primary purpose of learning to read.

Check It Out

The Big Book of Phonics Fun (Greensboro, NC: Carson-Dellosa, 1994). This book is a terrific collection of phonics games and other activities. It's filled with lots of ideas to add variety to phonics lessons.

Phonics They Use: Words for Reading and Spelling, 2nd ed., by Patricia M. Cunningham (New York: HarperCollins, 1995). The phonics activities are fun (tongue twisters are used for letter-sound awareness, for example) and are based on solid research.

Teaching Phonics Today: A Primer for Educators by Dorothy S. Strickland (Newark, DE: International Reading Association, 1998). A simple, straightforward monograph on teaching phonics, written by one of the country's leading educators, this book provides a clear presentation of the phonics controversy in an easy-to-follow question-and-answer format.

HELPING YOUR STUDENT WITH WORD PATTERNS

Recognizing word patterns (sometimes called *word families*) is an important reading skill. Even very young readers are good at detecting word patterns. In fact, they're usually much better at word patterns than phonics or spelling rules. For example, if your student can read the word *pet*, then you can help your student discover that *met* and *set* follow the same pattern. Similarly, recognizing *pet* can lead to an understanding of how to read and spell *pen* and *peg*.

Tips for Tutoring English Language Learners

Word patterns can be particularly helpful for students who are learning English because the relationships between sounds and symbols are consistent. Be careful, however, to introduce words in meaningful contexts so that students learn what the words mean. Use pictures if necessary.

What to Teach

You can help your student learn basic word patterns by using the patterns below to make lists of rhyming words. (For example: *back, pack, sack; gain, main, pain, rain.*) In selecting word patterns, begin with patterns that have only one vowel and one consonant (*-at, -in, -it*) then introduce patterns with more vowels or consonants (*-ick, -ump, -ail*).

Did you know that 500 words can be built from the following 37 fragments?

-ack	-at	-ide	-ock
-ail	-ate	-ight	-oke
-ain	-aw	-ill	-op
-ake	-ay	-in	-ore
-ale	-eat	-ine	-ot
-ame	-ell	-ing	-uck
-an	-est	-ink	-ug
-ank	-ice	-ip	-ump
-ap	-ick	-it	-unk
-ash			

How to Teach Word Patterns

You can use the following sequence in planning a lesson that includes word patterns. Be careful about introducing too many patterns at one time, however; you don't want to confuse your student.

1. Start with a review pattern: *at, cat, hat, rat, sat, scat.*

2. Continue with a second review pattern: *art, Art* (note that this is a proper noun), *tar, star, stars* (point out singular and plural), *car, scar.*

3. Introduce a new pattern: *ash, cash, sash, rash, trash, crash.*

Your student will have more fun and learn more quickly if you use individual letters made of plastic or printed on small cards to move around. You can also make bingo, tic-tac-toe, or board games targeting specific words (see pages 108–111).

Word patterns lend themselves well to writing poetry. You may want to write a poem with your student using the word pattern for the day. Poems can involve an upcoming holiday or your student's interests.

Check It Out

Introducing Word Families through Literature (Greensboro, NC: Carson-Dellosa, 1994). This book is a fantastic resource for linking word patterns with children's books (K–3). For each word pattern, several children's books that use the pattern are recommended. The book also includes lots of additional reading and writing activities you can use to make teaching word patterns fun.

Making Words and ***Making Big Words*** by Patricia M. Cunningham and Dorothy P. Hall. (Parsippany, NJ: Good Apple, 1994). A complete guide to teaching word patterns, *Making Words* introduces word patterns to students in grades 1–3; *Making Big Words* is appropriate for students who are ready to read longer words (with multiple syllables, prefixes, suffixes, etc.).

HELPING YOUR STUDENT WITH SIGHT WORDS

All readers and writers need to develop a set of words they can recognize instantly. These are called *sight words.* Some English words are best learned by sight because they have no sound-symbol regularity; common examples are *there* and *one.* Other words occur so frequently that they should be known immediately; it's simply not efficient to sound them out.

What to Teach

You can help your student develop a bank of words to recognize quickly and easily. Your student's school or the materials used at your tutoring site may supply you with a list of words for your student to learn by sight. If you don't have a recommended list, you can use one of the sample lists found on pages 124–129. Compiled by well-known reading specialist Edward Fry, these lists of words that occur frequently in children's books are respected and widely used resources.

How many words should you teach during one tutoring session? That depends on the student's age, attention span, and tolerance for frustration, as well as the level of difficulty of the words. Start with three words per session and increase this number gradually, as time permits and as your student's interest allows.

How to Teach Sight Words

Here's how to start teaching sight words to your student:

1. Choose three words for your student to learn.

2. Write the first word on an index card.

3. Pronounce the word.

4. Ask the student to pronounce the word.

5. Talk about what the word means.

6. Work together to think of a sentence using the word. Write the sentence on the back of the index card.

7. Repeat steps 2–6 for the other two words.

8. At the end of the session, review all three words.

9. The next time you meet, flash the three words to your student. For each one read correctly, put a check mark on the index card. If your student misses a word, offer encouragement, read the sentence on the back of the card, and review the pronunciation and meaning of the word.

10. Add a few new words.

11. After a word gets five checks, you can enter the word into your student's personal dictionary (create this together using a notebook with one letter on each page, as described on page 71). Review the words in your student's dictionary from time to time.

Reviewing What You've Done

Most adults have forgotten enormous amounts of information they learned as children. Unused information quickly "disappears" from our memories. That's why review is an important component of effective teaching. Different students, of course, require different amounts of review. We suggest these general guidelines:

- Students of above-average ability may need fifteen to twenty exposures to a new word before it becomes a part of their long-term reading and writing vocabulary.

- Students of average or below-average ability may need thirty-five to sixty-five meaningful exposures.

Be patient. Don't get caught in the trap of thinking that if you taught it, your student has learned it. For many students, learning takes practice, review, and repetition.

HELPING YOUR STUDENT WITH LONGER WORDS

After students master basic phonics, word patterns, and sight words, the next step in learning to become a proficient reader is reading longer words—multisyllable words. If they are to become rapid, fluent readers, students must learn to recognize common prefixes, suffixes, and roots. This is the way most experienced readers tackle a longer word. For example, an adult reading *microorganism* might recognize the prefix *micro-* as meaning "very small," and the root *-organ-* as

meaning "alive," and the suffix *-ism* as indicating that the word is a noun.

For fun, test your own facility on the longest word in the English language (and you thought it was *antidisestablishmentarianism*): *pneumonoultramicroscopicsilicovolcanoconiosis.* Try to decipher this *before* checking an unabridged dictionary!

What to Teach

Teaching longer words includes teaching words containing prefixes and suffixes.

Prefixes. Prefixes are easier to teach than suffixes because their meanings are more concrete. It's often easiest to focus on prefixes first.

Common Prefixes		
PREFIX	MEANING	EXAMPLES
bi-	two	bicycle, binoculars
dis-	not	disagree, disappear, disobey
in-	into	inside, infiltrate
in-	not	incorrect, insincere
mis-	wrong	misspell, mistake
pre-	before	prefix, precede
post-	after	postwar, posterior
re-	again; anew	reread, rewrite
re-	back	return, retreat
sub-	under	submarine, subway
super-	above; over	superman, superior
trans-	across	transportation, transition
tri-	three	tricycle, triangle
un-	not	unhappy, untrue

Suffixes. When teaching your student suffixes, it's usually enough if the student learns to recognize the pronunciation of chunks (for example, *-tion* = /shun/) and can tell whether the suffix indicates a noun, verb, adjective, or adverb. Only suffixes with clear meanings (for example, *-ess* = woman, *-ful* = full, *-less* = without) should be taught during early stages.

Common Suffixes

Nouns

SUFFIX	EXAMPLES
-al	removal, approval
-ance	clearance, importance
-ence	absence, presence
-ity	stupidity, curiosity
-ment	excitement, argument
-ness	fairness, craziness
-sion	division, explosion
-tion	multiplication, addition, subtraction

Nouns That Refer to People

SUFFIX	EXAMPLES
-ent	student, president
-er	farmer, teacher, dancer
-ess	waitress, actress
-ist	artist, cartoonist
-or	sailor, actor

Verbs

SUFFIX	EXAMPLES
-en	strengthen, weaken
-ify	beautify, glorify
-ize	summarize, capitalize

Adjectives

SUFFIX	EXAMPLES
-able	moveable, drinkable
-ful	careful, thoughtful
-ic	artistic, gigantic
-ive	creative, active
-less	careless, thoughtless
-ous	curious, religious
-y	curly, shiny, leafy

Adverbs

SUFFIX	EXAMPLES
-ally	naturally, totally
-ly	slowly, quickly

How to Teach Longer Words

When teaching prefixes and suffixes, work on only a few at a time. Here are some additional tips:

- The most effective approach is to teach each prefix in the context of several words. *Example:* Teach *dis-* in *disagree, disappear,* and *disobey.*

- Be sure that the words you choose are good examples. *Example:* For teaching *in-* as the opposite of *out-, inside* is a good example while *incorrect* is not.

- Present each new word in a sentence pair that focuses on its meaning. *Example:* "I *agree* with you. She *disagrees* with you."

Check It Out

The Reading Teacher's Book of Lists, 3rd ed., by E.B. Fry, J.E. Kress, and D.L. Fountoukidis (Englewood Cliffs, NJ: Prentice-Hall, 1993). This is the best resource for lists of word patterns, prefixes, suffixes, roots, and other reading-related lists.

HELPING YOUR STUDENT READ AND RESPOND TO STORIES

Have you ever come out of a movie muttering, "The book was so much better"? When people read a story, they create the world of the book in their minds. They envision the setting, identify with the characters, and respond with empathy, anger, excitement, joy, sadness, or fear. The story comes alive, and the reader gets to "live" in someone else's head for a time.

Most of what children read, especially in the early grades, is stories. Story reading continues throughout school. If you can help your student understand story structure and appreciate literature, you'll give your student a gift that will last a lifetime.

What to Teach

Because most children naturally like to hear stories, reading stories with a child offers a "teachable moment." For younger and less mature readers, story reading provides you an opportunity to teach concepts about books and print. Always start a story-reading session by identifying the title, author, and illustrator. As you read, you can reinforce print awareness by identifying letters, words, and punctuation marks.

You can also teach about story structure—the parts that make up a story. Story structure includes setting (time and place), characters (the people in the story), and plot (what happens first, second, next). Most stories have a problem or dilemma that gets resolved by the end of the story. Even young children can learn to identify the problem in a story and how it was resolved.

But these structural aspects aren't what hook people on stories; it's the personal reaction that does. Kids, like adults, connect to certain stories better than others, and they like to talk about their favorites. When you read stories with your students, budget time to discuss the story itself. Ask your students about their feelings about the characters and the action and their interpretation of the story. Be sure to model your own responses in talking about what you liked or didn't like about a particular story or character in the story.

Tips for Teaching English Language Learners

Students who are learning English may have difficulty comprehending stories for a variety of reasons. Their background knowledge and life experiences may be vastly different from what's represented in the story. That can make it very difficult for these students to understand a character's motives or reasons behind events. The story may also introduce new and unfamiliar vocabulary that the student needs to know in order to understand the story. The story structure, too, may be unusual and strange for them, or they may be more accustomed to an oral rather than a written storytelling tradition.

Think of lessons that focus on reading and responding to stories as a time to learn from each other. Plan enough time before reading to discuss what the student already knows about the topic, place, or period in history the story represents. Provide information about concepts that may be helpful to understand the story. Talk about new or unusual words (just a few) that may help comprehension of the story. During reading, take time to clarify new words and concepts. After reading, encourage your student to retell the story in his or her own words. You can even model retellings from time to time.

How to Teach Story Reading

Sometimes it's easier to help your student understand and respond to stories when you read them aloud. Beginning readers can struggle with comprehension, given the variety of reading tasks they are still mastering. As students progress in their reading skills, however, they become more able to read independently. The following suggestions can be used whether you and your student read aloud or silently. The Guide for Story Reading on pages 81–82 can also structure your story-reading sessions.

1. Get ready. Before reading, think about ways to get your student involved with the story. If the story is set in a place or time that is unfamiliar to your student, bring out the atlas or encyclopedia and help your student establish where and when the story takes place. If the story contains unfamiliar vocabulary or concepts, introduce them at the beginning to help your student prepare. This will aid comprehension.

2. Get set. After reading the first few pages or chapters (either orally or silently), talk about the main character in the story. Try to get your student involved with the characters and their situation. Help your student imagine what he or she would do in a similar situation and try to relate the characters and their circumstances to his or her own life.

3. Go. Read the rest of the story or read the book chapter by chapter. Stop occasionally to summarize what is happening and to talk about personal reactions.

4. Cool down. Immediately after reading the story, talk with your student about personal reactions to the story. What parts of the story were most enjoyable? What parts of the story were least enjoyable? Also talk about the author's style of writing. What words, phrases, or images struck your student? What would your student do if he or she were one of the characters?

5. Follow up. Think about how your student can respond to the story through art, writing, drama, cooking, or perhaps by reading another book from the same genre or by the same author. See Fifty Fantastic Ideas for Book Sharing, pages 111–112, for many ideas.

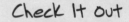

Check It Out

Read It Again! series by Liz Rothlein and various coauthors (Glenview, IL: GoodYear Books). This series of books provides teaching suggestions for children's books related to specific themes. Themes in the series include multiculturalism, environmental issues, and individuals with disabilities. Each book in the series provides lesson plans for different children's books. This is an excellent resource for launching story-sharing activities.

Response Journals: Inviting Students to Think and Write About Literature by Julie Wollman-Bonilla (New York: Scholastic, 1991). This short but powerful book includes specific suggestions for helping students respond to stories through writing.

Story Stretchers: Activities to Expand Children's Favorite Books and *More Story Stretchers* by Shirley C. Raines, Robert J. Canady (Washington, DC: Gryphon House, 1990, 1991). These books connect 180 of the best children's books to other learning areas—science, nature, math, art, music movement, cooking and circle time. They are especially geared toward teaching primary-grade students.

HELPING YOUR STUDENT READ AND RESPOND TO INFORMATIONAL TEXT

Informational or expository text is designed to teach—to provide information about a topic. Science, social studies, and health textbooks and encyclopedias are examples of informational text. So are newspapers, menus, handbooks, and instructions. Informational text is frequently loaded with new concepts, vocabulary, and facts. Often, students are required not only to read this information, but also to retain it for tests and class discussions. Quick, superficial reading won't do. Rather, students need to practice reading more slowly, with learning in mind.

What to Teach

The most effective method of teaching students to understand informational text includes four basic components:

1. Prereading helps students focus on the topic to be read. Chances are, if you're reading a science passage about cell division, your student is thinking about anything *but* cell division. Students need to learn how to preread in order to understand and retain the material. When prereading, students quickly preview the chapter, think about what they already know about the topic, and then try to predict what they are going to learn.

2. Comprehension monitoring is active reading. Have you ever read an entire page of a textbook and then thought to yourself, What did I just read? Comprehension monitoring involves keeping track of what you understand and what you don't. When mature readers don't understand a passage, they try to stop and "fix things up" so they can continue reading. Teaching comprehension monitoring helps students become active readers by helping them notice when they don't understand what they are reading and teaching them "fix-up" strategies. Teach students to ask themselves questions as they are reading and to go back and reread early on if they don't understand.

3. Summarizing during reading is another way to keep track of your understanding along the way. As you read a section of a chapter, you might think to yourself, What is this mostly about? What are the key ideas here? If you don't understand, you might go back and reread, especially if you have to take a test on the material. Summarizing can also involve taking notes to record key ideas to study later.

4. Summarizing after reading helps students prepare for tests. After reading a chapter, a student can think, What are the most important ideas of this whole chapter? What does the teacher want us to learn? This kind of reflection after reading helps students identify key ideas to review.

How to Teach Informational Text Reading

Teaching comprehension of informational text takes some patience. Start with short passages that will hold your student's interest. That way, you can keep your student engaged while teaching important strategies for understanding. Here are some suggestions for helping your student become more systematic when reading informational text.* The Guide for Reading Informational Text on pages 83–84 can help you structure sessions with your student.

1. Preview the reading assignment. Look at the pictures, the headings and subheadings, the introduction, and any summaries. Try to predict what the assignment is about.

2. Talk briefly about the topic. Ask your student what he or she already knows about the topic and what he or she expects to learn by reading the passage.

3. Break up the reading assignment into a few short sections (headings and subheadings should help).

4. Read the first section with your student—either silently or aloud, whatever seems most appropriate.

5. Talk about words, sentences, or ideas that seemed difficult or confusing to your student (the "clunks").

6. Work together to think of ways to fix the clunks.

7. Ask your student to tell you the key ideas from the section you read.

8. Read the next section. Once again, talk about clunks and key ideas.

9. After reading the whole assignment, talk about the most important ideas that your student has learned.

10. Take turns predicting questions that the teacher might ask on a test.

11. Think together about what else you would like to learn about the topic.

This procedure takes some time, but it's worth the effort. By following these steps, your student can learn how to link new information to what he or she already knows, "fix up clunks," and identify the most important ideas in a passage. Remember, you're helping your student develop strategies to read and study more efficiently and effectively.

Check It Out

Improving Reading: A Handbook of Strategies by Jerry L. Johns, Peggy VanLeirsburg, and Susan J. Davis (Dubuque, IA: Kendall/Hunt, 1994). This book is great for teaching any of the reading areas covered in this chapter. It's a practical tool that you will refer to again and again.

Questioning the Author: An Approach for Enhancing Student Engagement with Text by Isabel L. Beck, Margaret G. McKeown, Rebecca L. Hamilton, and Linda Kucan (Newark, DE: International Reading Association, 1997). This book outlines an exciting strategy, Questioning the Author, to help students become more engaged with the author's message as they read. This is a valuable resource for those interested in promoting lively discussions during tutoring sessions. The strategy can be used with either narrative or expository text.

---

*This procedure is an adaptation of Collaborative Strategic Reading, a strategy developed by J.K. Klingner, S. Vaughn, and J.S. Schumm. *Elementary School Journal* 99 (1998): 3–22.

Guide for Story Reading

Step 1: Get Ready

- Read the title page.

- Skim through the book looking at illustrations.

- Answer these questions:

  What is the title of the story? _____

  Who is the author of the story? _____

  Who is the illustrator of the story? _____

  What is the setting of the story? _____

      Time in history: _____

      Place: _____

  What do I predict this story will be about? _____

  _____

  _____

Step 2: Get Set

- Read the first few pages or first chapter.

- Identify the main characters in the story.

- Answer these questions:

  Who are the main characters in the story? _____

  _____

  _____

  What do you know about these characters? _____

  _____

  _____

continued →

Guide for Story Reading continued...

Step 3: Go

- Read the rest of the story or the next chapter.

- Stop from time to time while reading to summarize what is going on and how you react to the story.

Step 4: Cool Down

- Think about what you read.

- Answer these questions:

What were the key events that happened in this story? _____

_____

_____

What part of the story did you like best? _____

_____

_____

What part of the story did you like least?_____

_____

_____

Would you recommend this story to a friend? Why or why not? _____

_____

_____

Step 5: Follow Up

Think about how to follow up with this book. _____

_____

_____

Guide for Reading Informational Text

Reading assignment: _____

Topic: _____

Step 1: Preview

- Look over pictures, charts, and graphs.

- Quickly read the introduction, headings, subheadings, and summary.

- Answer these questions:

  What do I know about this topic? _____

  _____

  What do I think I'm going to learn about this topic? _____

  _____

Step 2: Action Reading

- Read the assignment, one section at a time.

- After each section, identify and fix up "clunks" (difficult or confusing words or ideas).

- List two or three key ideas.

  Section 1:

  Clunks: _____

  Key ideas: _____

  _____

  Section 2:

  Clunks: _____

  Key ideas: _____

  _____

continued →

Section 3:

Clunks: _____

Key ideas: _____

_____

Section 4:

Clunks: _____

Key ideas: _____

_____

Step 3: Wrap Up

- Think about the whole passage you read.

- Talk about the most important ideas.

  Most important ideas: _____

  _____

  _____

  _____

  _____

  _____

- Predict five or six questions the teacher might ask on a test.

  _____

  _____

  _____

  _____

  _____

  _____

A B C D E F G H I J K L M N O P Q R S T U V W X Y Z

The creation of a thousand forests is in one acorn.
—Ralph Waldo Emerson

CHAPTER 8

MEETING SPECIAL WRITING NEEDS

Ron hated writing. It wasn't that he didn't have anything to say; he just had a terrible time putting words down on paper. Writing caused trouble for him in almost all his classes. He took part in class-room discussions and knew the material, but his responses on essay questions were brief and indeci-pherable—even to Ron. He had a very hard time writing clearly and quickly and often just gave up even before the time was up.

Tutor Janey Lowe helped Ron by spending fifteen minutes each week working on writing. She showed Ron a more comfortable way to hold his pencil and focused first on printing legibly. She modeled free writing and spoke aloud as she wrote, illustrating the

transformation of the words in her head into words on the paper. Janey and Ron planned time to do writing activities, which helped his writing become more fluid. At the end of each session, Ron evaluated his own writing for clarity of thought and readability. He set his own goals for the next lesson. Janey also began teaching Ron how to use a keyboard so he could write assignments on a word processor.

After four months of work, Janey showed Ron something that really surprised him—a sample of his writing from their first day together. He was stunned. "I can't believe how far I've come," he said. "I can read my own writing now, and my teachers can, too."

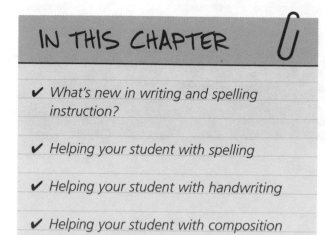

In addition to helping students with reading, you can help them become better writers. Writing is important for success not only in school, but also in the world of work and daily life.

WHAT'S NEW IN WRITING AND SPELLING INSTRUCTION?

Writing instruction has gone through major changes in most schools in the United States since the early 1980s. Understanding these trends in how writing is taught will help you better tutor your student. With your support and encouragement, these new ways of teaching writing can help students grow into adults who write well and actually *enjoy* writing.

An Emphasis on Substance First

Educators today teach writing as a process that emphasizes meaning. The purpose of writing is to convey a message to the reader. Only after a student gets his or her content, or ideas, down on paper do teachers shift the focus to nice handwriting and correct spelling and grammar. Teachers guide students through the writing process from prewriting to drafting to editing, and they move on to polishing the students' writing

only when it has a purpose. This process reflects the way people write in real life. Some writing—a note to a family member, for example—doesn't need to be polished; the message just has to get across. Other writing, such as a cover letter requesting a job interview, must have impeccable spelling, grammar, and neatness.

Probably the most important thing you can do when tutoring writing is to be your student's best audience. Really read and listen to your student's writing. Focus on ideas first—try to appreciate what your student is communicating. Think of ways to share your student's writing with a wider audience, and point out specifically what your student does well.

A Greater Understanding of Developmental Spelling

Children progress through stages of temporary spelling much like they progress from crawling to walking and from babbling to speaking understandably. Teachers now know that a child who spells *love* "l" has made progress from spelling it as a squiggle or heart, and they know how to nudge to get *lv, luv,* and eventually *love.*

Your students (especially younger students) may talk about *invented spellings.* Their teachers might encourage them to write what they hear and spell it the best they can. This is important for early stages of spelling development because it helps students think about the relationships between sounds and symbols. But students also need specific instruction in standard English spelling.

You can encourage your student to use invented spellings when writing informally. Invented spellings are perfectly appropriate for the dialogue journal (see pages 52–57)—after all, its purpose is conversation. And you can also work to nudge students toward standard English spelling.

Tips for Teaching English Language Learners

Encourage students who are learning English to invent spellings while writing in their dialogue journals and in their first drafts of writing. Not only will you give them practice in expressing themselves through writing, but you'll also learn about their knowledge of phonics and vocabulary in examining their invented spellings. Work on standard spelling at another time, but model standard spelling in your own writing.

Less Use of Grammar and Composition Textbooks

In many classrooms, the grammar and composition textbook is becoming more of a reference book and less of an everyday text. Writing instruction tends to stem from real writing. Rather than focusing on grammar exercises from a textbook, your students may learn principles of grammar by viewing pieces of writing on an overhead projector and exploring the concepts in their own writing. The rationale is that when students learn grammar through composition, they better see the purpose for their learning. Endless repetition of a concept or rule that a student already understands is busy-work. Tutoring lets you serve as a personal writing coach, helping your student improve by zeroing in on individual needs.

More Attention to Student Choice

The trend toward making writing instruction more meaningful goes hand in hand with the trend toward offering students more choice in learning. If a writing assignment is purposeful and makes sense to students, they are more likely to learn. Some teachers let students choose their own spelling words, which probably include words students actually want to learn for their own writing. Other areas where students are offered choice include the types of writing students do (essays, poems, short stories, play scripts) and the topics they write about. Such freedom can be difficult for some students, however, especially those who are reluctant writers or those who can't decide on a topic.

You can help your student learn to make choices and plan compositions based on those choices. You'll find some suggestions for helping your student make choices about what to write in Writing Ideas from A to Z on page 92.

More Student Involvement with Assessment

Traditionally, it's the teacher's job to assess writing and assign grades. While this is still the case, students are encouraged to be more involved in evaluating their own work. Peer editing, or students providing feedback on each other's writing, has become common in many schools. Similarly, self-assessment—each student thinking about areas of strength in his or her own writing and areas that need improvement—is also encouraged. Peer editing and self-assessment are considered key parts of the writing process. As a tutor, you can help your students learn how to evaluate their own writing and also how to use constructive feedback to set personal goals. (See the A-OK editing checklists on pages 100–101 for a way to give your students feedback and help them evaluate their own writing.)

HELPING YOUR STUDENT WITH SPELLING

As many people learning English as a second language can testify, learning to spell in English is not easy. Many languages, such as Spanish, have more consistent spellings than English. What you hear is what you spell. Because English has "borrowed" so many words from other languages, it contains many irregular spellings.

When your student writes in your dialogue journal with you, neither of you should worry about the student's spelling. Journaling is for sharing ideas. In writing for other audiences, however, spelling can be important. Spell-checking software isn't foolproof, so learning how to spell standard English is important for success in school, at work, and in social situations. In our society, standard spelling is a mark of education.

What to Teach

The teaching of spelling is closely related to the teaching of reading. A typical spelling curriculum includes learning to spell *regular words* (words that follow rules of sound-letter correspondence), *irregular words* (the exceptions to the rules), words every reader should know on sight, basic word patterns, and longer words (using prefixes, suffixes, etc.).

Keep in mind that the younger the student and the more difficulties he or she has with spelling, the fewer words he or she can learn at one time. For some students with LD, learning three new words a week would be challenging. Start small with a few words, learn them well, and then gradually increase the number of words you teach at one time.

Also remember that the younger the student and the more difficulties he or she has with spelling, the more repetitions he or she will need to remember how to spell a word. Patience is important.

How to Teach Spelling

Chapter 7 includes many activities you can use for teaching both reading and spelling. The ideas included in the sections on the relationships between sound and letters, sight words, word patterns, and reading longer words (pages 72–77) work well for spelling as well as reading.

Weekly spelling tests are a time-honored tradition. While spelling programs differ from school to school and from class to class, many teachers still give weekly spelling tests. Here's how you can help your student prepare for spelling tests.

Pretest. On the day spelling words are given, test your student on these words. Determine which words your student knows and which ones he or she needs to study. For the latter, note what *parts* of the words your student already knows.

Set up a study schedule. Determine when you'll be available, and then help your student plan for studying alone or with a parent or friend when you can't be there. (See the Sample Spelling Study Schedule on page 90.) Write the schedule down, including what words the student will study on what day. This is particularly effective if parents can help.

Practice. Use a variety of methods to help your student practice. Here are several you can try:

- Ask your student to write each word five, ten, or fifteen times.

- Let your student type the list on a computer and use spell-checking software. Play with fonts and sizes.

- Write each word in large letters. Ask your student to trace the words with a finger and pronounce the word while tracing. Repeat until he or she can write the word from memory.

- Dictate each word to your student. Then have him or her correct the spelling. This encourages close attention to mistakes.

- Record the words on tape, leaving enough time between each word so your student can write it. Your student can use the tape for practice when you're not around.

- Try the Word Pairs game on page 89.

Word Pairs

This game can help you teach new words to your students. It works best for relatively simple words.
Use this method for up to three words a day. Follow the steps below for each new word.

STEP	WHAT TO SAY	WHAT TO DO
1. Look at the word.	"First we're going to look at the word. Let's look at the word _____."	Show the word and pronounce it.
2. Listen to the beginning sound.	"The first game we'll play is about the beginning sound of the word. I'll say four words, and you show me with thumbs up or thumbs down if the word begins like _____."	Say four words—three that have the same beginning sound as the target word, one that is very different.
3. Write the beginning spelling.	"Now we'll play another beginning sound game, but this time you'll write it. I want you to write the beginning sound of the word _____."	Have the student write the beginning of the word. If the student makes an error, compare it with the model you showed the student in step 1.
4. Listen to the rhyme.	"The next game is about the ending sound of the word. I'll say four words, and you show me with thumbs up or thumbs down if the word ends like _____."	Say four words—three that have the same rhyme as the target word, one that is very different.
5. Write the rhyme.	"Now we'll play another ending sound game, but this time you'll write the ending sound of the word. I want you to write the ending sound of the word _____."	Have the student write the end of the word. If the student makes an error, compare it with the model you showed the student in step 1.
6. Say the word slowly and fast. (This teaches segmentation and blending.)	"In the last game we'll look at the different sounds that make up the word. First, I want you to listen as I read the sounds of the word slowly."	Put the target word in front of the student. Put a dot under each key letter sound.
	"Now I want you to say the word slowly like I just did, naming the sounds that make up the word as I point to the dots and say the word."	Say the sounds while pointing to the dots on the model. Have the student say the sounds and read the word slowly.
	"Now say all the sounds quickly. Read the word quickly."	Have the student say the sounds and read the word quickly.
7. Write the word.	"Now I want you to write the word without looking."	Remove the model and have the student write the word on a blank card. If the student isn't successful, repeat steps 1–6.

Adapted from J. Gordon, J.S. Schumm, and S. Vaughn. "The Effects of Phonemic Training on the Spelling Performance of Elementary Students with Learning Disabilities." (Coral Gables, FL: University of Miami, 1993).

When you practice spelling with your student, offer feedback letter by letter rather than word by word. For some students, learning to spell is *very difficult.* Spelling a whole word can be tough. Celebrate each letter of a word spelled correctly, and then give suggestions for the letters that are not correct.

For example, if the target word is *clear* and your student spells it *cer,* you might say to your student: "Good for you! You got the beginning letter *C* and the ending letter *R.* You also got the right vowel sound. You remembered that every word needs a vowel. You got three of the letters right! Let's work on two more. The beginning sound has a little more to it. It has the *C* just like you wrote, but it also has an *L.* Listen as I say the beginning sound. Now you say the beginning sound. Now write the beginning sound. Good. The word *clear* also has a vowel you can't hear. Look at the word—what is the vowel you can see, but you can't hear? It's an *A*— good for you. Now, let's try writing the word *clear* again."

Sample Spelling Study Schedule

Monday (with tutor)
1. *Tutor gives student a pretest on the whole list, noting correct and incorrect parts of words not yet mastered.*
2. *Tutor helps with the three or four most difficult words on the list.*
3. *Tutor tests student on all the words learned so far.*

Tuesday (at home)
1. *Student reviews all the words learned so far and two new words.*
2. *Student tests self on all the words learned so far.*

Wednesday (at home)
1. *Student reviews all the words learned so far and two new words.*

2. *Student tests self on all the words learned so far.*

Thursday (with tutor)
1. *Tutor tests student on all words learned to date.*
2. *Tutor and student practice the most difficult words.*
3. *Tutor tests student again.*

Friday—*Spelling test day!*

Check It Out

The Alphabet Superhighway
http://www.ash.udel.edu/ash/

This Web site sponsored by the U.S. Department of Education's Read*Write*Now! initiative has an excellent resource called the Wild World of Words. Students can do word games and figure out crazy word combinations and unusual origins. It also has great interactive spelling resources for students at several levels.

Moving On in Spelling by Cheryl Lacey (New York: Scholastic Professional Books, 1994). This book offers excellent spelling activities to add variety to your spelling lessons. The author also provides sound advice for giving students feedback on their spelling and for integrating spelling instruction with reading and composition.

Spelling Book: Words Most Needed Plus Phonics for Grades 1–6 by Edward Fry (Laguna Beach, CA: Laguna Beach Educational Books, 1992). This is a fantastic tutoring tool, particularly if your student doesn't have a set spelling curriculum. It tackles simple to complex words and concepts, including sight words, phonics, word patterns, and irregular words.

HELPING YOUR STUDENT WITH HANDWRITING

Handwriting is difficult for many children (and adults, too). The process of writing by hand can feel laborious, and many people now turn to computers for writing ease. Even though computers are becoming prevalent at school and at home, students still complete most schoolwork by hand, and legible handwriting remains an important tool for communication and success in school.

There are many reasons why students may have difficulty in writing so others can read it. Here are a few:

- The student may not be interested in handwriting.

- The student may not recognize that legible writing is an important means of communication.

- The student's fine motor skills may be developing more slowly than those of other students.

- The student may have a specific learning disability, *dysgraphia*, which makes writing very difficult, even when the student knows how to read and spell orally.

- Left-handed students may have trouble positioning the paper and gripping a writing instrument to write comfortably. Plus, because their writing hand often covers what they've already written, they may need more help in monitoring their handwriting.

- The classroom structure doesn't allow enough time to practice handwriting in class.

As a tutor, you can show your student how clear handwriting helps communicate ideas. You can also provide practice exercises to help your student's handwriting skills improve. With firm and caring assistance, even the most reluctant writer can learn to write more legibly.

What to Teach

In the early grades, students typically learn *manuscript writing*, or what is commonly called printing. Students learn about

- the shapes of letters, both capital and lowercase
- the sizes of letters
- the spacing of letters within and between words

In later grades, usually starting in third grade, students learn *cursive writing*, or script. Schools differ widely in the emphasis placed on cursive writing—some insist that students use only cursive; others allow more choice. Like printing instruction, the curriculum for cursive writing emphasizes the shape, size, and spacing of letters, but also includes the proper slant (tilted to the right).

How to Teach Handwriting

There are many ways to help your student improve handwriting. Mostly it takes practice. Check with your student's teacher first to see what style of handwriting your student is learning in school because there are several different styles. Get a sample, if possible. The Zaner-Bloser printing and cursive charts (see pages 130 and 132) are the ones most commonly used in U.S. schools. Pages 131 and 133 also include practice paper you can reproduce to help your student with printing and cursive writing.

Here are guidelines you can use to plan practice sessions:

- Allow ten to fifteen minutes for practice.

- Teach a few letters at a time. These are your "target letters."

- Start with lowercase letters—they're used more frequently.

- Spend a few minutes reviewing letters learned in previous sessions.

- Practice the target letters for the day.

- Practice the letters in real words. Choose words carefully so your student can practice the new letter at the beginning, the middle, and the end of words.

- Encourage students to evaluate their own handwriting, rating their own size, shape, spacing, and other features. See How's My Printing? and How's My Cursive? on pages 93–94.

- Keep practice brief and try to make it fun. Bring colored pencils, crayons, and various other writing instruments.

HELPING YOUR STUDENT WITH COMPOSITION

Writing is usually taught as a process involving these steps: prewriting, organizing, drafting, revising, and sharing or "publishing." Students, impatient to complete a written assignment, are often satisfied with just one draft. As a tutor, you can help your student become a better writer by teaching patience and by emphasizing the steps in the writing process. Students who learn the value of the prewriting-drafting-revising process find their writing greatly improved, no matter what kind of writing they're doing.

What to Teach

Teaching composition can be fun if you can get your student to start thinking as an "author." Tara, a six-year-old girl, asked Jeanne (one of the authors of this book) what she did, and Jeanne responded, "I'm an author. I write books." The girl replied, "I'm an author, too!" Tara's mom said, "She's right—Tara wrote four books at school."

Tara's teacher inspired her to start thinking as an author. Tara thought of her writing as real books—books her family and friends would be interested in reading. Tara "published" her books and put them in a final form with a cover, title page, and illustrations. Her four books are now treasured volumes in the family library.

Writing Ideas from A to Z

A	ad, advice column, autobiography	**N**	newspaper, notice, nursery rhyme
B	bedtime story, brochure, bumper sticker	**O**	obituary, ode, ordinance
C	cartoon, cereal box, CD cover	**P**	party plan, play, postcard
D	diary, directory, drama	**Q**	quiz, questionnaire, quotation
E	editorial, e-mail message, encyclopedia entry	**R**	recipe, rhyme, riddle
F	fable, fashion article, fortune	**S**	sign, song, sports story
G	game rule, graffiti, greeting card	**T**	TV program, thank-you note, travel brochure
H	headline, horoscope, how-to article	**U**	up-to-the-minute news story, urgent notice
I	infomercial, interview, invitation	**V**	villanelle, visiting card, vivid verbs
J	job description, joke, journal	**W**	weather forecast, Web site, wish
K	keynote speech, kiddie story, knock-knock joke	**X**	X-ray results
L	legend, letter, limerick	**Y**	yarn, yearbook
M	menu, movie review, mystery	**Z**	zany tale, Zen koan, zoo map

How's My Printing?

Name _____ Date _____

Today's letters _____

Rating Scale:

1 = great

2 = good

3 = needs more work

Letter size   _____

Letter shape   _____

Spacing within words   _____

Spacing between words   _____

My goals for next time: _____

_____

_____

_____

_____

_____

_____

_____

How's My Cursive?

Name _____ Date _____

Today's letters _____

Rating Scale:

1 = great

2 = good

3 = needs more work

Letter size   _____

Letter shape   _____

Letter slant   _____

Spacing within words   _____

Spacing between words   _____

My goals for next time: _____

_____

_____

_____

_____

_____

How to Teach Composition

Here are five steps to follow in taking your students through the writing process:

Step 1: Prewrite. Before beginning to write, students need to identify their intended *audience:* Are they writing for themselves, classmates, a close friend, or a teacher? They also need to be clear about the *purpose* and type of writing they are doing: Are they writing a story, writing to provide information, or writing to persuade? To help your student think about these issues, use the Story Planner on page 97 and Informational Writing Planner on pages 98–99. If you want to explore different formats, Writing Ideas from A to Z on page 92 can get you started. (You and your student can use a dictionary to look up any of the ideas you're unfamiliar with.)

One effective way to help your student with prewriting is through brainstorming—generating and listing ideas without restriction. Classrooms, organizations, and businesses across the county use brainstorming to promote creative thinking and problem solving. You can participate in brainstorming with your student as long as you both play equal roles. A brainstorming session is not the time to exercise authority or to insist that your ideas are the "right" ones.

Brainstorming has two simple rules:

- Generate as many ideas as possible—from serious to outrageous and everything in between. Try to use those ideas as springboards to come up with new ones. As the noted American chemist Linus Pauling said, "The best way to have good ideas is to have lots of ideas."

- Accept all ideas during brainstorming. Don't criticize or praise any ideas at this point. Save the weeding out for later.

Some people like to use a brainstorming technique called *freewriting,* or writing whatever comes to mind nonstop for two or three minutes. Other people like to brainstorm out loud, talking with friends and jotting down the ideas that come up. If your student's writing skills aren't at the point where he or she can write quickly, you can take responsibility for recording ideas.

You can help your student brainstorm possible topics to write about, ideas to include in a composition, lists of information your student already knows about a topic, or even possible resources for finding more information.

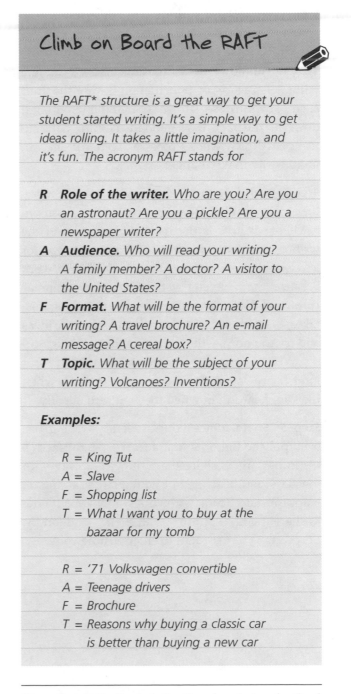

Climb on Board the RAFT

The RAFT* structure is a great way to get your student started writing. It's a simple way to get ideas rolling. It takes a little imagination, and it's fun. The acronym RAFT stands for

R   Role of the writer. *Who are you? Are you an astronaut? Are you a pickle? Are you a newspaper writer?*

A   Audience. *Who will read your writing? A family member? A doctor? A visitor to the United States?*

F   Format. *What will be the format of your writing? A travel brochure? An e-mail message? A cereal box?*

T   Topic. *What will be the subject of your writing? Volcanoes? Inventions?*

Examples:

R = King Tut
A = Slave
F = Shopping list
T = What I want you to buy at the
      bazaar for my tomb

R = '71 Volkswagen convertible
A = Teenage drivers
F = Brochure
T = Reasons why buying a classic car
      is better than buying a new car

---

*From *Content Reading Including Secondary Systems* by Carol Santa (Dubuque, IA: Kendall Hunt, 1988).

Step 2: Organize. Once writers have generated enough ideas, they can go through and organize them. They can begin crossing off ideas that don't fit and grouping the ideas that do into a logical order. A formal outline may not be necessary, but they should try to arrange the details of the composition in some kind of sequence and cluster like ideas together. (Planner sheets to help writers get organized are included on pages 97–99.)

Step 3: Write the first draft. After determining the general sequence of ideas, the writer can create a first draft. Some people call this the "sloppy copy." Writers shouldn't worry too much about the fine points of spelling or punctuation during the draft stage. The purpose is to get something (anything!) down on the page. It's a good idea for the writer to use pencil or a word processor so he or she can more easily make changes later on.

Step 4: Revise. Not only do revisions take patience, they also require attention to detail. Classroom teachers say this is the most difficult part of the writing process to teach. It's hard for younger or less-experienced writers to revise their own work because they haven't yet internalized grammar rules, and they may not see their own spelling mistakes. It's even harder to help them look at the ideas and try to improve the content of their writing.

Whenever possible, writers should read out loud for revision. Errors are easier to catch when they are heard than when they are read silently.

Step 5: Share. Once your student's writing has been polished into its final form (or "published"), it's important to share the writing, not only with the classroom teacher, but with a larger audience, if appropriate. Think with your student about how to share the final product with friends and family. Encourage your student to enter writing contests.

A-OK Editing

The A-OK method is one way to make revising easier and more efficient. It helps students focus on one aspect of writing at a time. Introduce it by modeling, taking your student through each step of the method and showing how it's done. Eventually your student will be able to revise more independently.

A-OK has five steps (four for younger writers):
1. MOK (Meaning OK)
2. POK (Paragraph OK)
3. SOK (Sentence OK)
4. WOK (Word OK)
5. NOK (Neatness OK)

At each step, the student asks questions to evaluate his or her writing. The amount of revising necessary depends on how your student answers the questions. The A-OK steps are presented as checklists with full instructions on pages 100–101: one for beginning writers and one for more advanced writers.

Story Planner

Title of story _____

Author _____

Setting

Time _____

Place _____

Characters' names

1._____ 2._____

3._____ 4._____

5._____ 6._____

Problem _____

_____

_____

_____

_____

Solution _____

_____

_____

_____

_____

Informational Writing Planner

Topic _____

Author _____

Introduction _____

_____

_____

_____

_____

_____

_____

_____

_____

_____

_____

Main idea #1 _____

_____

Supporting details

1. _____

_____

2. _____

_____

3. _____

_____

continued ⟶

Informational Writing Planner continued . . .

Main idea #2 _____

_____

Supporting details

1. _____

_____

2. _____

_____

3. _____

_____

Main idea #3 _____

_____

Supporting details

1. _____

_____

2. _____

_____

3. _____

_____

Summary and conclusion _____

_____

_____

_____

_____

A-OK Checklist for Beginning Authors

Title _____

Author _____

MOK (Meaning OK?)

☐ Does it make sense?

☐ Are my facts correct?

☐ Did I say what I really wanted to say?

SOK (Sentence OK?)

☐ Does it express a complete thought?

☐ Does it start with a capital letter?

☐ Does it end with the correct punctuation mark?

WOK (Word OK?)

☐ Is it the very best word?

☐ Is it spelled correctly?

☐ Is it capitalized correctly?

NOK (Neatness OK?)

☐ Is it easy to read?

☐ Does it follow the format required by my teacher?

A-OK Checklist

Title _____

Author _____

MOK (Meaning OK?)

☐ Does it make sense?

☐ Is it concise and to the point?

☐ Is it complete?

☐ Are my facts correct?

☐ Did I say what I really wanted to say?

☐ Is there an introduction?

☐ Is there a conclusion?

POK (Paragraph OK?)

☐ Is it indented?

☐ Is it made up of sentences related to one main idea?

☐ Is it connected logically with paragraphs that come before or after?

SOK (Sentence OK?)

☐ Does it express a complete thought?

☐ Does it start with a capital letter?

☐ Does it end with the correct punctuation mark?

☐ Do the subject and verb agree?

WOK (Word OK?)

☐ Is it the very best word?

☐ Is it spelled correctly?

☐ Is it capitalized correctly?

NOK (Neatness OK?)

☐ Is it easy to read?

☐ Does it follow the format required by my teacher?

Check It Out

"Think & Grin"
Boys' Life
Boy Scouts of America
1325 Walnut Hill Lane
Irving, TX 75015-2079

Publishes jokes written on postcards. Ages 8–17.

Child Life
1100 Waterway Blvd.
Indianapolis, IN 46206

Publishes short stories (1,000 words) and poetry. Ages 10–12.

Cricket Submissions
Carus Publishing Company
315 Fifth Street
P.O. Box 300
Peru, IL 61354
(815) 224-6656
http://www.cricketmag.com

A children's magazine that considers young people's poetry, art, and stories for contests and publication. Submissions must be accompanied by a statement signed by a teacher or parent assuring that the child's work is original and that no help was given. Ages 7–14.

New Moon: The Magazine for Girls and Their Dreams
P.O. Box 3587
Duluth, MN 55803-3587
http://www.newmoon.org

This magazine publishes letters, news about girls and women, "herstory" articles about girls and women from the past, articles about girls and women of today doing great things, letters about unfair things that happen to girls just because they're girls, reviews, poetry, drawings, quotes, and more. Submission guidelines on the Web. Ages 10–15.

Shoe Tree: The Literary Magazine By and For Children
P.O. Box 452
Belvidere, NJ 07823

A quarterly published by the National Association for Young Writers, "Helping Children Write to the Top." All stories, poems, and artwork are done by children. Holds annual competitions for young writers in fiction, poetry, and nonfiction. Ages 5–14.

Skipping Stones
P.O. Box 3939
Eugene, OR 97403-0930
(541) 342-4956
http://www.nonviolence.org/skipping/

An international children's magazine that encourages an understanding of different cultures and languages, with an emphasis on ecology and human relationships. Includes artwork, writings, riddles, book reviews, news items, and a pen pal section. Ages 8–18.

Stone Soup
P.O. Box 83
Santa Cruz, CA 95063
(408) 426-5557
http://www.stonesoup.com/

"The magazine by young writers and artists," which publishes stories, poems, book reviews, and art by children and adolescents. Submission guidelines are available on the Web. Ages 8–13.

National Written & Illustrated By . . . Awards Contest for Students
Landmark Editions, Inc.
1402 Kansas Ave.
Kansas City, MO 64127

Publishes books by young authors in three age categories: 6–9, 10–13, 14–19. Each entry must be written and illustrated by the same student. For complete rules and guidelines, send a self-addressed, stamped, business-size envelope with two first-class stamps.

Tyketoon Young Author Publishing Company
7414 Douglas Lane
Fort Worth, TX 76180

Publishes approximately one book each year by a young author at each grade level from 1–8. Authors and illustrators receive cash scholarships paid as a royalty on each book sold.

Giving Your Student Feedback

Some students—like many adults—are very sensitive about their writing. Perhaps insecurity, shyness, fear of failure, or past criticism have made students reluctant to share what they've written. But it's difficult to grow as a writer without getting feedback from readers. Educator Nina Zaragoza has developed a procedure she calls *TAG* for giving feedback that lets the writer know his or her work is valued and provides suggestions in a gentle and productive way:*

T—Tell what you like. Give writers specific examples of what was good about their composition. "Your introduction was powerful. It really got me interested," or "The character Timmy is funny. I'm eager to read what he's going to do next," or "The description of your bedroom was vivid. I could picture it in my mind." Be specific about what you liked and try to give at least three examples.

*From "Process Writing for High-Risk and Learning Disabled Students" *Reading Research and Instruction* 26 (1987): 184–193.

A—Ask questions. Try to discover what students were thinking when they were writing. You might ask, "I'm curious about why you decided to use the jungle as your setting. Can you tell me more about it?" The purpose is to get students to talk more about their writing and some of the decisions they made while writing.

G—Give suggestions. Give one or two suggestions for improving the written piece. Don't give too many suggestions—you'll overwhelm your students. You might also ask young writers to provide suggestions as well. This is a good time to set personal goals for revision.

Share your own writing with your student. Perhaps you've written a poem, a story, or a letter. Serving as a writing role model can demonstrate that writing is important in everyday life and in the world of work. Make certain that you give your student the opportunity to respond to your writing using TAG—Tell what you like, Ask questions, Give suggestions. You'll find yourself becoming a better writer, too!

Check It Out

A Fresh Look at Writing by Donald Graves (Portsmouth, NH: Heinemann, 1994). This book offers practical suggestions for implementing writing as a process and for encouraging student writing in different genres.

25 Mini-Lessons for Teaching Writing by Adele Fiderer (New York: Scholastic Professional Books, 1997). Here is a great resource for helping your students work on specific aspects of their writing such as writing a snappy introduction or a conclusion with a bang. These ten-minute lessons will fit well in your tutoring sessions.

*What is really important in education is not that the child learns this and that,
but that the mind is matured, that energy is aroused.*

—Søren Kierkegaard

CHAPTER 9

MAKING YOUR TUTORING SESSIONS LIVELY

Max Brown tutors eight-year-old Travis every Tuesday over lunch. Because Travis has a different tutor each day of the week, the program at the school is highly materials driven; in other words, the tutors practically follow a script.

"After three months," says Max, "I was impressed with the progress Travis was making. The program was paying off. But Travis was getting bored with the routine." Max asked the tutor coordinator if it would be OK to stop each session five minutes early to try some other reading and writing activities. Once he got the green light, he implemented his plan: He selected one of Travis's favorite books—one with a predictable pattern to the text—and read it aloud with Travis. Instead of pointing out specific words as he had done before while reading

this book, Max drew Travis's attention to the "formula" or pattern of the text itself. He then suggested that Travis use that formula to write his own book. Together they brainstormed text to fit into the established pattern—and no idea was too wild, to Travis's delight. Over a period of several weeks, Max patiently guided Travis through all the steps of the writing process, then had Travis illustrate his book as well. He brought in a colorful photo album with magnetic pages in which Travis could paste and "publish" his story.

Max's experiment was highly successful—both he and Travis looked forward to the new activity. And the tutor supervisor asked Max and Travis to share their activities with other tutors at the next tutor-training session.

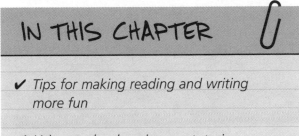

IN THIS CHAPTER

✔ Tips for making reading and writing more fun

✔ Using technology in your tutoring sessions

✔ Using games in your tutoring sessions

Have you ever taken dancing lessons? If you have, chances are the first step you learned was the box step. Step—together, step—together, step—together, step—together. The box step is the basis for many other dance steps, and it's a good way to start learning to dance. But after a while, it's limiting.

Likewise, when you begin tutoring, it's good to start with a routine. A set routine helps you and your student become familiar with the basics of a tutoring session before you get rolling. But after a while, you'll need to shake things up.

This chapter offers many ideas you can use to add variety and fun to your sessions. What you choose to do will depend on your student's interests and needs, as well as your skills and the equipment and materials you have available. Use these ideas as prompts for your own imagination and creativity. You may want to take note that while such ideas add fun to tutoring sessions, these hands-on activities also are important learning techniques, especially for students who are more kinesthetic learners—those who learn best by doing.

TIPS FOR MAKING READING AND WRITING MORE FUN

Read a book, write a book report—does anyone really enjoy doing that? Here are ten tips for making reading and writing more exciting! Work with your student to think of even more.

1. Read something other than books. Bring in newspaper stories, catalogs, magazines, menus, scripts for plays, recipes, and even comic books.

2. Make 'em laugh. Students need a belly laugh to brighten their day. Find joke books, riddles, and funny stories to share with your student. Laughter is a great way to brighten your student's day—and yours.

> ### Check It Out
>
> **The Little Giant Books.** *Jokes* by Joseph Rosenbloom, *Riddles* by Joseph Rosenbloom, and *Knock-Knocks* by Charles Keller (New York: Sterling, 1997). These books may be small, but they deliver big delight with hundreds of laughs and groans for kids of all ages.

3. Write a book with your student. Work through the stages of the writing process—prewriting, organizing, drafting, revising—to produce a finished book you can "publish" and share. You can purchase blank books to fill in together, bind loose pages at a copy center to make your book, or create your own special homemade binding.

4. Integrate art with your reading and writing. Students can illustrate their own writing or respond to their reading through drawing or other media.

5. Integrate music with your reading and writing. If you're reading a biography of Louis Armstrong, Mozart, or Selena, bring in a recording of the music. If you're reading about Louisiana, play some Cajun music. Play different types of music softly while your student is writing—you may be surprised to see how the tone of the music affects the tone of your student's writing.

6. Link reading and writing activities to holidays and other special events. Students look forward to breaks in their regular schedules. As holidays approach, find related books to share with your student. Plan writing activities like making cards or writing letters or stories to commemorate the special day.

7. Make books and stories come alive for your students. Dress up as a character from a book you are reading. If that's not your style—or if your glass slippers are in for repair—collect props mentioned in the story, make a mask of a character, or use puppets to animate storytelling. The more tangible you make the experience, the more interesting and memorable the session will be to your student.

8. Practice following written directions. You can have fun while teaching an important skill by doing an interesting activity together. You can learn together by assembling a model, following a recipe, tying balloons into animal shapes, or any number of things. Check out craft and activity books—preferably ones with clear, easy-to-follow instructions and illustrations—for a wealth of ideas.

9. Do a "quickie." Short, one-shot learning activities can energize both you and your student. Need some ideas? Here are some resources for five-minute activities:

Check It Out

Jump Starters by Linda McElherne (Minneapolis: Free Spirit Publishing, 1998). These brief, meaningful, enjoyable activities can help you start a tutoring session off right, cure the blahs, or end a session on a positive note.

Take Five by Charles Mangrum II and Eugene F. Provenzo (North Billerica, MA: Curriculum Associates, 1996). This little book is a collection of high-interest, low-materials activities that can be completed in five minutes. It includes great suggestions for teaching reading and writing skills.

10. Advertise your student's success. The two of you work hard together, and you're making progress. It's time to let other people know. Toot your own horn! Think of ways to let parents, grandparents, teachers, and anyone else know what's going on. You can make a scrapbook, newsletters, flyers, ads, certificates—you name it.

Tips for Teaching English Language Learners

Expert teachers of students who are learning English recommend using reading material that students are likely to encounter in their daily lives. Here are twenty suggestions:

1. *baseball cards*
2. *cereal boxes*
3. *menus*
4. *catalogs*
5. *record/cassette/ CD labels*
6. *movie ads*
7. *greeting cards*
8. *toy labels*
9. *horoscopes*
10. *letters from pen pals*
11. *recipes*
12. *food labels*
13. *street and building signs*
14. *gum or candy wrappers*
15. *travel brochures*
16. *comic strips*
17. *T-shirts*
18. *bumper stickers*
19. *coupons*
20. *lyrics to popular songs*

USING TECHNOLOGY IN YOUR TUTORING SESSIONS

In this book, we've defined literacy as being able to read and write. But learning to be "computer literate" is also important, and you might want to help your student with these skills, too. As Eugene Provenzo, a University of Miami professor specializing in technology in education, puts it: "Computers represent a turning-point time in our culture that is as profound as the invention of the printing press was to late fifteenth-century Europe. Just as the printing press and the printed book defined the Renaissance, the computer is defining our own era."

Computers affect not only how we communicate with each other, but also how we teach reading and writing. The influence of computers is growing, but students and classrooms today vary widely in their access to equipment and supplies, software and supplementary materials, and training in using technology to help meet learning goals.

Integrating technology into your tutoring sessions can mean more than using computers and the Internet. Video recorders, videotapes, audiotapes, fax machines, digital cameras, and other kinds of equipment can also add novelty to your time with your student.

You've already read about materials-driven tutoring programs. In some cases, the materials include computer software. If your tutoring site uses such a computer-driven program, then you're likely to receive training in the program itself as well as in your role in monitoring student progress and supplementing instruction.

Because most tutoring programs don't involve using specific software, this section will focus on how you can integrate whatever technology you have available into your tutoring sessions. Following are three basic guidelines:

1. Use what you already know.
2. Use what equipment is available to you.
3. Focus on your student's learning goals.

With those guidelines in mind, consider these ten ideas you can use to jazz up your sessions with technology. Work with your tutor coordinator and your student to generate other ways to enliven your sessions with technology.

1. Skill and drill. Some software programs provide structured practice in reading and writing, very much like filling in worksheets. Choose software that fits the goals of your student and supports the instructional plan you are following. Even on computers, skill-and-drill lessons can be boring. Short practice sessions are preferred.

2. Games. Like skill-and-drill programs, instructional games and video games need to be examined carefully. While the game's promotional material may say it teaches spelling, you still need to determine what skills, level, and pacing the program incorporates. Keep your instructional purpose in mind when choosing games.

3. Hypertext and hypermedia. Have you ever read a textbook and encountered an unfamiliar word or concept? You might have thought, I should look that up in the dictionary or an encyclopedia. Sometimes you take that extra step, sometimes you don't. Many Web sites and CD-ROMs have those extra steps built in. As you read about volcanoes, for example, you can click on links for definitions of key words or concepts (hypertext). Perhaps you can even click in a video presentation of famous volcano sites (hypermedia). Using hypertext or hypermedia materials can supplement book reading activities in exciting ways. It encourages students to be active readers and to seek additional information when they run into "clunks"—new ideas and concepts they don't understand.

4. Word processing. You can use word processors for a variety of purposes in your tutoring session: writing compositions, practicing spelling words, writing letters to parents, and completing homework assignments. Because the program you use may be different from the one your student uses at home or at school, check first to find out what your student has been learning. Avoid teaching new programs that are drastically different—it can cause confusion.

5. Desktop publishing. After your student has brainstormed, drafted, and revised a composition, you can use desktop publishing programs to help your student prepare a final polished product. Seeing their own writing designed and printed can really motivate students.

6. E-mail. If you and your student both have e-mail, you can use it to communicate between sessions. You can use e-mail as the vehicle for your dialogue journal or to help your student keep in touch with parents, teachers, or e-mail "key pals."

7. The Internet. The Internet offers a whole new world of reading and writing opportunities. You can use the Internet to generate reading material for your tutoring sessions or help your student do research for a school report. Search for sites that focus on your student's interests or topics from class. If you have the time, equipment, and inclination, you can also create a Web site with your student.

8. Videos. The number of films based on books is staggering. Although your goal is to help your student learn to read and appreciate books, videos can help motivate students to read. You can use a videotape to engage your student in a story. Watch the first fifteen or twenty minutes of the video to help your students visualize the characters and setting; then begin the story with your student. Watch a video after reading a book or story and talk about the decisions the director made in translating the story to film. You probably won't have time to view an entire tape during a tutoring session, but you can identify key scenes ahead of time and view those scenes with your student.

9. Videotaping. In addition to watching videotapes, you can create your own. Videotape your student reading aloud and present the tape to your student's parents. They will be amazed at their child's progress in reading.

10. Faxing. Students love to receive mail. They also love to receive faxes. Sending and receiving faxes can give students a real purpose for writing and reading. They might have fax pals, or they might send faxes to businesses or organizations requesting information for a personal project. Do they want to write a letter to an author they admire? They can fax the publisher a letter to forward to the author.

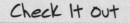

Check It Out

Teachers, Computers, and Curriculum: Microcomputers in the Classroom by Paul G. Geisert and Mynga K. Futrell (Boston: Allyn & Bacon, 1995). Each chapter includes suggested activities and recommendations for software.

If you need more up-to-date information, professional journals are a great source of instructional ideas. Here are a few that you may find helpful:

Electronic Learning
902 Sylvan Ave.
Englewood Cliffs, NJ 07632

Teaching K–8
P.O. Box 54808
Boulder, CO 80322-4808
http://www.teachingk-8.com

This monthly professional magazine has a web site that offers resources and teaching ideas.

USING GAMES IN YOUR TUTORING SESSIONS

One sure way to make your tutoring sessions fun is to play games. Although games provide relief from routine, they can also steer you away from your goals and objectives. Games designed to reinforce your lessons, however, can be a great use of your tutoring time. Here are some guidelines for making games an integral part of your tutoring plan:

1. Emphasize participating, not winning. Your student's goal should be to compete with himself or herself, not with you. If your student gets discouraged because you always "win," find a different kind of game.

2. Select games that are designed to teach. Some games are simply fun and can help you get to know your student. If that's your goal, such games are fine. But remember, you are responsible for helping your student learn to read and write. Try to find games that build rapport and teach at the same time.

3. Make certain the games you use are consistent with what you are teaching. Choose games that will reinforce your student's learning. For example, Scrabble can help improve spelling, but does it focus on the spelling skills you are teaching your student at the time? If not, you might want to create your own game instead.

4. Save games until the end of the session. This gives your student a treat to anticipate. If you promise a game, though, make sure you leave enough time to play it.

5. Keep learning goals in mind as you play. But also try to have fun. This is a great time to giggle and to learn.

Guidelines for Constructing Games

Some of the best games of all are those you make for your student. When you can't find a game to reinforce a specific skill your student needs to master, you can make one yourself—with your student's help. Here are some general tips for making your own learning games:

■ Choose a specific learning goal, and don't try to incorporate too many goals into one game.

■ Don't spend more time making the game than your student will spend playing it. (Depending on its purpose, you may only use it once or twice.)

■ Get your student involved in the game-making process. This can be a fantastic problem-solving opportunity.

■ Brainstorm together to create an imaginative name or theme for the game.

■ Have plenty of materials on hand—scissors, construction paper, cardboard, markers, rulers, etc. Use stickers, rubber stamps, pictures from magazines, comic strips, or coloring book pages to decorate the game.

■ Write down the rules. Not only does this prevent future conflict, it also models writing.

You can adapt many familiar games to your student's interests and tailor them to skills he or she needs to practice. On page 134, you'll find game "cards" that you can copy. You can also use paper and pencil or chalkboard and chalk for most of these games.

Bingo

Materials:

Poker chips, pennies, or bits of paper for space markers

Bingo cards (see page 134)

Flash cards or bingo numbers

Rules:

1. Call out a question or flash a flash card.

2. If your student provides the correct response, draw a bingo number, call it out, and have your student put a marker on the corresponding space.

3. Play continues until your student gets BINGO—five markers in a row either horizontally, vertically, or diagonally.

Ways to play:

Learning letters: Write lowercase letters on the bingo cards. Make flash cards of corresponding uppercase letters. Flash a card and have your student match it to a letter on the board. *Variation:* Have your student match cursive and manuscript letters.

Learning vowels and vowel sounds: Label the five columns on the board with A-E-I-O-U rather than B-I-N-G-O. Call out a word. When your student correctly identifies the vowel sound, he or she can place a marker in any square in that vowel column.

Learning sight words: Write the words you've chosen in the squares on the bingo board. Say them aloud, one at a time, while your student covers each word he or she recognizes.

The Matching Game

Materials:

Pairs of flash cards you create out of paper or index cards. Each card you make must have a match.

Rules:

1. Shuffle the cards, then arrange them individually facedown in a square or rectangle.

2. To take a turn, a player turns over any two cards.

3. If the cards match, the player removes them and takes another turn.

4. If the cards don't match, the player places them facedown in the spaces from which he or she picked them up, and the next player takes a turn.

5. Play continues until all matches have been made. The player with the most matches wins.

Ways to play:

Learning sight words: Make card sets using sight words that you want to teach. Have your student read the word out loud when he or she finds both cards.

Learning vocabulary words: Make card sets that match a word with its definition.

Learning synonyms (*small, tiny*), **antonyms** (*small, big*), or **homonyms** (*there, their*): Make card sets using these kinds of words.

Card Games

Materials:

Homemade playing cards you create out of paper or index cards. Each card you make must have a match.

Rules:

Follow the rules of Go Fish. Players are dealt a set number of cards, and the remaining cards are laid facedown in a stack. Players lay down any matching pairs. In turn, each player asks the next player for a specific card in hopes of making another match, laying down any matches that are made. If the next player has no match, he or she says, "Go Fish," and the first player must draw a card from the deck. The turn passes to the next player.

Ways to play:

You can use your homemade cards to help your student learn the following:

- rhyming words (*blue, shoe*)
- compound words (*rowboat*)
- vocabulary words and their definitions
- words and their abbreviations (*Doctor, Dr.*)

Hangman

Materials:

Paper and pencil or chalkboard and chalk

Rules:

1. Explain that the object of the game is to identify an unknown word, starting with only the number of letters.

2. Think of a word, then draw a space for each letter on the paper or chalkboard.

3. Players try to figure out the word, guessing one letter at a time. If the letter is found in the "mystery word," write it in the appropriate blank space (or spaces). If the letter is not in the word, draw a body part for the hangman. *Hint:* Agree from the start on which body parts you'll draw to complete the hangman. To avoid losing, some students will want to add everything from eyelashes to toenails.

4. To win, a player must identify the mystery word before all the hangman's body parts are drawn.

Ways to play:

Learning spelling words: Work from the current week's spelling list—and throw in some review words.

Learning vocabulary words: The student defines the word after identifying it.

Board Games

Board games can be used to practice almost anything, from sight words to word patterns. You don't have to make board games from scratch to create ones that meet your goals for your student. You can use the boards from games you already have if you tie taking turns to answering questions, reading vocabulary words, or recognizing sight words. It's easy to design your own Reading Pursuit, Spelling Pursuit, or Vocabulary Pursuit. If you don't have board games that you think will work for these purposes, you can create your own.

Folders from drugstores, discount stores, or office supply stores can make great board games. The picture on the folder can set the theme for the game. For example, a folder with a baseball pitcher on the front can become Syllable Strike-Out, or a folder that pictures cats can become Capitalization Cat-Nap. Most folders are blank inside, so you can use this blank surface to draw the game board upon. Draw a path with crayons or felt-tipped pens, and be sure to include special squares with instructions such as *Start, Go Back 3 Spaces, Go Forward 2 Spaces,* and *Draw a Card.* If the folder has a pocket, use it for storing place markers, rules, game pieces, score pads, and other materials used to play the game.

Use your student's interests to make the game more fun. If your student is a sports fan, draw a football, soccer, or baseball field instead of a path. Your student earns yardage, goals, or base hits with every correct answer. Or you can make your board in the shape of a favorite cartoon character, a musical instrument, a car, and so on.

You can use homemade board games to test almost anything—from sight words to vocabulary, root words to spelling.

The time you spend with your student can and should be special. Once you get to know each other, agree on ground rules and procedures, and set up routines, you'll both be anxious to move on to fresh ideas. Use the ideas in this chapter as starting points for new ideas of your own.

Tutors succeed when they incorporate their own talents and skills into tutoring sessions. Maxine Milton, an artist, creates art projects to tie in with books she reads with her student. Cliff Hendry, a guitarist, puts his student's poetry to music. Matt DeFuniak, a computer wizard, introduces his student to the World Wide Web and e-mail. Ileana Diaz, mother of six, uses board games to teach because her own children love games. Don't be afraid to use your own style and flair. It's what will make you very special to your student.

Fifty Fantastic Ideas for Book Sharing*

1. List ten characters in the book.
2. List five characters and next to each name, write the character's occupation.
3. How old do you think the main character is? Why? Name three things the character does that match that age.
4. If you could meet one of the characters, who would it be? List five questions you'd like to ask him or her. What answers do you think you'd receive?
5. Choose a character who made an important decision. Describe the incident.
6. Describe the foods and drinks that one character might have for lunch.
7. List five characters from the book. Give each a nickname and tell why you chose it.
8. Find an example of stress or frustration. Tell about it. How did the character resolve it?
9. Do you think the main character would like a job at a local fast-food restaurant? Why or why not?
10. Would you choose the main character as your best friend? Why or why not?
11. Pick your favorite character. Give at least three reasons for your choice.
12. Pick your favorite and least favorite characters in the book. Give reasons why these characters could or could not be your friends.
13. Write a letter of advice to one of the characters.

---

*Adapted from L.A. Blanchfield. "Fantastic Activities for Book Sharing." *Florida Research Quarterly* 4 (1991): 32-33. Used with permission.

14. Dress up as one of the characters or make a mask of the character.

15. Bring in props mentioned in the book and put on a play.

16. Your favorite character has just been granted three wishes. (None of the wishes may be for more wishes.) Tell what those wishes would be.

17. It's your favorite character's birthday. What gifts would you bring to the party?

18. Your favorite character just bought a T-shirt. Draw a picture of the T-shirt. Explain the picture.

19. One of the characters has a problem. Describe it and tell how it was solved.

20. Make a diary entry that your favorite character might write.

21. Act out various scenes in the book.

22. Make a video about one of the scenes in the book. You may have friends and family help with this assignment.

23. Pick seven events that happen in the book and write them on a time line or draw them in a cartoon strip.

24. List five events that happen in the book in chronological order.

25. Write a follow-up chapter for the book.

26. In what season does the book take place? Give supporting statements.

27. Would you like to live in the setting (time and place) of this book? Why or why not?

28. List different kinds of transportation mentioned in the book.

29. Use a blank world or U.S. map to locate settings in the book.

30. Compare or contrast objects found in the book to what we have today.

31. Find examples of feelings in the book—love, guilt, honesty, trust, loneliness.

32. Find an example of humor in the book.

33. Survey ten students from your class. Ask them two opinion questions about the book. Record your results.

34. Write a poem about the book.

35. Write a rap about the book.

36. Write a song about the book.

37. Read your favorite part as if you were a radio announcer. Tape record your reading.

38. If your book were made into a movie, who would you choose to play the various roles? You may pick friends or famous people.

39. Read a selection from the book to two friends and one family member. Write about their reactions.

40. Make up a dozen questions and answers about the book. Make a board game using the questions.

41. Make up three essay questions that would be good for the end of the book test.

42. Tell the book's publisher or author what you think about the book.

43. Make up ten interview questions you'd like to ask the author.

44. Make up a new title for the book. Why did you choose it?

45. Make up a title for each chapter.

46. Look up the author in a reference book. Tell five things you learned about this person.

47. Keep a Wonderful Word List. When you come to a new word or a nifty saying or phrase, write it down.

48. Find three examples of onomatopoeia (words that resemble the sound, like *moo, hiss, cluck, slam*).

49. Draw a picture of the house (or other dwelling) where the main character lives.

50. Come up with your own activity!

When we seek to discover the best in others,
we somehow bring out the best in ourselves.
—**William Arthur Ward**

CHAPTER 10

EVALUATING AND TROUBLESHOOTING

Sarah Young, a freshman in college, volunteered to tutor at a local middle school. She was thrilled to have the opportunity to work with kids and think about something other than her regular studies. The reading specialist at the school assigned Sarah to Whawn, a sixth grader who was reading on a second-grade level.

When Sarah first met Whawn, he seemed cool and distant. Sarah was certain he'd warm up after a few sessions together, but after three weeks, she became frustrated. Whawn wouldn't participate in their tutoring sessions, no matter what she tried. When she tried to discover his interests, he simply didn't respond. He was sullen, sarcastic, and resis-

tant to any ideas Sarah offered. Sarah told the classroom teacher and the school reading specialist that she felt Whawn just didn't like her. Both professionals encouraged Sarah to keep trying, but even after a few more weeks, nothing improved. Finally, Sarah asked the reading specialist if she could talk with Whawn's mother.

Whawn's mother confirmed Sarah's instincts: For whatever reason, Whawn didn't like Sarah. He didn't mind being tutored, but the chemistry between the two just didn't work. The reading specialist assigned Whawn to another tutor and Sarah to another student. Everybody was more comfortable with the new arrangement.

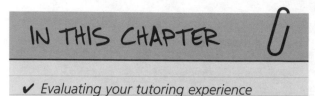

IN THIS CHAPTER

✔ *Evaluating your tutoring experience*

✔ *Frequently asked questions*

Ongoing evaluation of your sessions is important, not only for your student, but also for yourself. Your evaluation and conversations may help you identify areas you can sharpen and improve, as well as help you track your effectiveness. The troubleshooting section, "Frequently Asked Questions," includes common concerns tutors have, and helpful recommendations.

EVALUATING YOUR TUTORING EXPERIENCE

No program is complete without evaluation. The most effective tutoring programs include not only careful planning and training, but also ongoing evaluation that allows you to adjust your sessions along the way, and a final evaluation to guide future planning.

Your tutoring program may include a comprehensive evaluation program. If so, participate—register your joys and your concerns. If not, you'll need to initiate this step in order to get as much as possible out of the experience. Here are some things you can do to evaluate your program on an informal basis:

Keep a tutoring journal. At the end of each session, reflect on what happened during the session. Think about things that went well, questions you need to ask another tutor or your tutor coordinator, ideas for upcoming sessions, and your short-range and long-range goals. You can track your student's progress as well as your own evolution as a tutor by reading through earlier journal entries.

Keep lesson logs to track tutoring sessions. (See page 41 for forms you can use.) Lesson logs are more structured than a journal, but they serve a similar purpose. You can fill out the lesson logs by yourself or with your student. Look over your logs periodically to get a clearer picture of your progress, and talk about your observations with your tutor coordinator.

Reflect on your sessions with your student. At the end of each session, talk with your student about how the session went. The Reflections form on page 115 can guide you and your student in talking about what he or she learned, what you both liked, what was confusing, and what you could change.

Reflect on the tutoring program with other tutors. Organize "joys and challenges" sessions or go for coffee with other tutors to learn from each other and do some creative problem solving. Avoid the temptation to complain about students or tutoring policies in a lounge area or on the phone with other tutors.

Meet periodically with your tutor coordinator. Discuss what's working in your tutoring sessions and get help troubleshooting problems you face.

Evaluation can guide you to address areas that need more attention and work. It can also help you discover that you are touching your student's life in ways you didn't expect and encourage you to articulate what you are gaining from the experience.

Reflections

Name of student _____ Date _____

What I learned today _____

_____

_____

_____

Something that was confusing today _____

_____

_____

One thing I liked about the lesson _____

_____

_____

One thing I would change about the lesson _____

_____

_____

One goal for our next time together _____

_____

_____

FREQUENTLY ASKED QUESTIONS

The tutoring stories and other examples in this book are largely positive, because mostly good things happen when you help teach someone to read and write. There are rough spots along the way, but with common sense and sensitivity, you can navigate these bumps and potholes—if not avoid them. The following questions address some of the most frequent "bumps" tutors encounter.

"I tutor in a school. It seems that every time I go there, the class is taking a standardized test or exploring outside on a field trip, and my help isn't needed. One day I walked into the school just as Smoky Bear came through the front door. Assembly time! The problem is, I never know ahead of time. The teacher knows I drive through traffic to get here. Why isn't he more considerate of my time?"

Teachers are busy, and their primary focus is on their students. While this may not be a good excuse for your teacher's lack of planning and communication, it's reality. Even though schools have a calendar of events, events can pop up on the school schedule without warning, and sometimes teachers don't know in advance. Make sure you have a copy of the school schedule, and ask the teacher about any special events that may be scheduled during your next visit. It's frustrating to show up only to find your session canceled. Do your best to prevent that by asking the right questions, but understand that sometimes surprise conflicts are out of the teacher's control.

"Theresa is my student. I've been asked to help her with reading and spelling very simple words. After five weeks of working with her, she still can't seem to remember one thing I've taught her. I think she has a learning disability. Should I tell her parents?"

Unless you're trained in assessing LD, attention deficit disorder (ADD), dyslexia, or other reading disorders, you're unqualified to make that diagnosis. Most tutors aren't experienced diagnosticians and shouldn't assume that role—formally or informally. Nor should you be the first to recommend formal testing. Labeling a student learning disabled can produce alarm and confusion in the student and his or her family. Talk with your tutor coordinator about your observations. Your role is to bring potential problems to the attention of a professional. Theresa may need to be tested for a potential learning difference, but others are in a better position to assess her needs.

"Cara started out with a bang. She learned so many new words and sounds I couldn't believe it. Now she seems to have come to a standstill. I just don't see much progress anymore."

If you've ever gone on a diet, you may have discovered that when you first start out, you often drop pounds quickly. Then nothing happens. You seem to have hit a wall. Likewise, it's not unusual for students who are learning to read and write to hit plateaus—periods of even performance with little or no progress. As with a diet, it's best to be patient. Stick with your plan and keep providing your student with reasonable challenges. Don't be afraid to take some risks and try something new if you think it might nudge your student forward. But don't get discouraged. Your student will start moving soon enough.

"Mickey just won't listen. I spend most of our time together trying to rein him in. After I leave the tutoring session, I'm bushed. I don't know whether I even want to come back. This isn't what I signed up for."

Remember, you have the right to help with problems you encounter during tutoring, and you don't have to face behavior problems in isolation. Ask for help and guidance.

In general:

- If you've followed your tutoring program's guidelines for establishing behavior standards, and

- If you've set up ground rules for your tutoring sessions, and

- If you've communicated those rules and consequences to your student, and

- If you've consistently implemented and followed these rules and consequences, and

- If your student still can't or won't behave,

- THEN this is not what you signed up for.

Although it can be hard to admit that things aren't going as you expected, you need to take responsibility for asking for help. Talk with the tutor coordinator at your site using the TACT strategy (see the box on this page): *Tell* your coordinator what's gone well in your sessions and what hasn't. *Ask* what he or she thinks about your experience with your student and get concrete suggestions on how to respond. *Collaborate* and communicate with everyone involved to address your concerns, providing specific instances and examples of your student's misbehavior. *Tie* the conversation up with an action plan that you develop in cooperation.

The action plan may outline steps you might take to improve the situation. Practice them ahead of time before your next session. Or maybe the action plan you come up with involves assigning you to another student. Perhaps your student isn't the best candidate for tutoring or would respond better with another tutor. Different students have different needs. Don't consider this a failure.

Communicating with Key Stakeholders: The TACT Strategy

*When you work individually with a student, you gain special insights about your student's strengths and challenges that others may not be able to see. You'll collect information about your student's progress in meeting goals as well as areas where your student needs more help overcoming challenges. From time to time, you'll need to share your observations and insights with key stakeholders: your student's teachers, parents, your tutor coordinator, and other professionals. The **TACT** Strategy can help you give parents and other key stakeholders your insights in a sensitive manner to serve your student's best interests. TACT represents a sequence for conferences:*

T Tell *something good about your student. Think of one, two, or even three of your student's specific accomplishments, positive work habits, or social skills. Starting out with dilemmas, problems, or predicaments can get you off on the wrong foot.*

A Ask questions. *Ask the stakeholders what they think is going well and what concerns they have.*

C Collaborate *to identify one or two areas that need improvement. Concentrate on addressing those areas with key stakeholders. Don't try to cover too much territory in one session; you'll get overwhelmed.*

T Tie *things together at the end. Summarize key ideas you discussed and determine an action plan. Schedule a time to meet again if necessary. Finally, leave the meeting with a positive thought about the student.*

"Doreen has an attitude. She just doesn't want to meet with me. I think she doesn't like me, but her mom and the tutor coordinator at my site tell me not to worry."

This situation pops up from time to time in tutoring partnerships. Typically, when well-constructed routines are in place and activities are geared toward the student's interests and needs, the "attitude" goes away.

As a rule, rearranging tutor-student partnerships can be disruptive. On rare occasions, like some of the examples mentioned earlier, tutors and students are mismatched and change is needed. This can happen for a variety of reasons. It just may not be the right match, the right time, or the right partnership for right now. Don't consider it a failure on your—or the student's—part.

"If he's told me once, he's told me a dozen times. Drew hates reading. As a matter of fact, he downright refuses to read. What can I do to jump-start this kid?"

Reeling in the student who hates to read is one of the most common challenges tutors face. Many students who hate to read (particularly in the upper grades) hate it for a reason. Reading has been hard for them to learn, they've faced humiliation because of a lack of reading skills, they've met with failure in school subjects, and they haven't been able to identify a real purpose—a real reason to read. Motivation is one of the most important building blocks of learning to read.

You can use the How I Feel About Reading interview questions on page 119 to uncover more concrete information about your student's attitude toward reading. Use that survey coupled with your Getting to Know You Interview (page 51) to identify interesting material at your student's independent reading level. Choosing materials that are compelling and readable is the first and best step.

Here are some additional ideas for motivating your student to read:

Don't just stick to books. Find other reading material that will match your student's interests and set a real purpose for reading (see page 105 in Chapter 9).

Before you read, help your student figure out the purpose. Whether it's to learn a new fact, find out how to do something, or learn about someone your student admires, define the reason. Set the purpose before you read and revisit it afterward.

Keep sharing practical purposes for reading. When students can see the reason for reading, they're more likely to get engaged.

Read out loud to your student. No matter how old he or she is, your student will benefit (see Chapter 6). Shared reading experiences help you serve as a role model for your student.

Use audiotapes. Get audiotapes of books that your student might enjoy and play them during your session, letting your student follow along in the book, perhaps.

Provide quiet times to read silently. Both you and your student can read at these times, whether you read the same material or you each pick something you find personally interesting. Start slowly. Read silently for only five minutes and then talk about what you read. Gradually add more time to your silent reading sessions—just one minute more per session, perhaps. Before long, you may be reading fifteen to twenty minutes or more.

How I Feel About Reading

1. What is reading? _____

_____

2. Are you a reader? Why or why not? _____

_____

3. What part of reading is very easy for you? _____

_____

4. What part of reading is more difficult for you? _____

_____

5. When you are at school, what's the *most* fun thing to read? _____

_____

6. When you are at school, what's the *least* fun thing to read?_____

_____

7. When you are at home, what's the *most* fun thing to read? _____

_____

8. When you are at home, what's the *least* fun thing to read? _____

_____

9. Do you like reading? Why or why not?_____

_____

10. What are three goals you'd like to set to improve your reading? _____

_____

_____

How I Feel About Writing

1. What is writing?_____

2. Are you a writer? Why or why not?_____

3. What part of writing is very easy for you? _____
- ☐ Handwriting?
- ☐ Spelling?
- ☐ Finishing assignments?
- ☐ Writing stories?
- ☐ Writing reports?
- ☐ Something else? _____

4. What part of writing is more difficult for you?
- ☐ Handwriting?
- ☐ Spelling?
- ☐ Finishing assignments?
- ☐ Writing stories?
- ☐ Writing reports?
- ☐ Something else? _____

5. At school, what's the *most* fun thing to write? _____

_____

6. At school, what's the *least* fun thing to write? _____

_____

7. At home, what's the *most* fun thing to write? _____

_____

8. At home, what's the *least* fun thing to write? _____

_____

9. Do you like writing? Why or why not? _____

_____

10. What are three goals you'd like to set to improve your writing? ____

_____

"Carlos is what you might describe as a reluctant writer. He just won't write. His teacher tells me that it takes him forever just to write two or three words on a page. It's killing him at school. Carlos and I have a good relationship, and I don't want to disrupt what we have going. But how can I get him to get his thoughts on paper?"

If you and your student have a good relationship, you might start with trying to find out *why* he or she doesn't like to write. Is it your student's handwriting? Does he or she write too slowly? Is he or she concerned about spelling? The How I Feel About Writing interview questions on page 120 can help you start a conversation about why writing is tough. Use your student's comments and concerns to develop mini-lessons during your tutoring sessions. The activities in Chapter 8 can help.

Generally, you can try to motivate reluctant writers in the following ways:

Offer support. Build their self-esteem; it may be quite fragile.

Start by talking. Encourage them to tell you stories out loud and react positively. Provide opportunities for them to record stories into a tape recorder so they can have the fun of listening to their own voices telling a story.

Try dictation. Let them dictate their ideas to you to get them on paper. This helps show concretely how ideas relate to written words.

Model fluent writing. Your dialogue journal is a good tool for this. Talk as you are writing to "think aloud" and model your thought processes during writing.

Use planning sheets to help students organize their writing. See the story writing and informational writing planners on pages 97–99.

Focus on meaning. Concentrate on their good ideas and the message they are conveying before stressing spelling and editing.

Begin with short assignments. Encourage students to complete short written assignments in a timely way, and then gradually increase the length.

Try to find a real audience. Writing for a genuine purpose helps students focus on communication.

Use a computer. Show students how to write a story on the computer; then use it to edit and check spelling.

Celebrate students' writing. Provide specific, sincere feedback remembering TAG: tell what you like; ask questions; give suggestions—and lots of praise!

"Hannah is really trying me. She insists on using foul language in her writing and in speaking to me. Frankly, I'm shocked that a fifth grader knows all these words."

Your student has succeeded. Her purpose was to test the limits and to shock you. Try using these suggestions to address the problem: First, ignore the inappropriate language. If the student's intent is to shock you and if the behavior isn't reinforced, it may eventually go away on its own.

If the behavior continues, discuss with your student the different levels of language that are appropriate for different audiences. You might say something like this: "People might use one level of very formal language in a court of law. We might use another level of language in the school. We might use still another level of language when talking with friends or in informal situations. The language you use in writing and in speaking to me should be the middle level—the language of school. I'm going to add 'We use school language in our writing and speaking' to our list of rules. If there are problems, then we'll follow our sequence of consequences." Be consistent.

"This is the third time I've canceled my tutoring appointment. The tutor coordinator at the after-school program was snippy when I called in to

explain that I couldn't come. I'm a volunteer, and she should understand that I do this when I can, but other things are going on in my life."

Maybe it's time to reevaluate your commitment to the tutoring program. If you find yourself canceling frequently, it may be that your motivation has diminished, other life priorities are more pressing, or the time is simply more inconvenient than you anticipated. Individuals who plan and manage programs depend on you. Your student depends on you. If you want to continue with the program, think about what changes need to be made. Otherwise, stop. Remember, your first responsibility as a tutor is to be there.

"I've attended every tutor training session my program has provided. I've also worked with children before, at camps. But I just don't feel I'm skilled enough to truly help Maureen."

Don't expect to be perfect. Don't expect to master all the diagnostic and remediation techniques that teachers with a graduate degree might have. Follow the steps you were provided in your training. Your job as a tutor is to provide practice and help keep students motivated. If you get to a point at which you aren't sure what to do, ask for help. Effective learners are effective help seekers. Some of the best tutors are those who ask questions—and actually, this book is the result of questions tutors have posed over the years. Keep tutoring. Keep asking. Keep learning.

"I just have this feeling that I'm not doing enough. I'd love to be there for Bart every day. He needs much more help than I can possibly give him in a few short hours. I feel bad that his school and his parents can't offer him more. I feel bad that I can't give more of my time. Bart deserves more than he's getting."

Think of it this way: What would Bart's life be like if his tutor didn't come at all? The contribution his tutor makes may not be *all* of what Bart needs, but

it is *some* of what he needs. Your example, support, and concern can make a difference in Bart's life.

Bart's situation may or may not change. But even at a very young age, he can learn two very important lessons from his tutor: First, a student like Bart can learn how to ask for help in appropriate ways. Talk with your student about the kinds of help he or she needs with reading and writing, who can provide him or her with help, and what times and ways to ask for help. Effective learners are those who can identify resources and use those resources to their advantage.

Second, you can teach your student independent learning strategies. When you teach your student a strategy—for example, how to study spelling words—think of ways that he or she can learn and study alone. Talk with your student about independent learning and work on those strategies during your tutoring sessions.

A Final Word

Even the most optimistic, patient tutors run into challenges with students. Chances are, you will too at some point during your tutoring experience. As the examples in this chapter reveal, many problems with students can be solved by making simple adjustments in your tutoring style or routine. As other examples show, some problems are more serious and require the help of your tutor coordinator or another professional. Remember that you have those allies to assist you when a problem seems out of your hands. Some situations are simply best corrected by changing the tutor and student combination.

The Reading Revolution has begun. Perhaps this book has motivated you to get involved and has equipped you with tools that will make your involvement productive and satisfying. The time you spend with your student—whether reading aloud, teaching reading strategies, or working through the writing process—is time well spent. Sometimes revolutions work slowly in strange, subtle, and simple ways. You are making a difference one student at a time, one day at a time.

APPENDIX

the	he	go	who
a	I	see	an
is	they	then	their
you	one	us	she
to	good	no	new
and	me	him	said
we	about	by	did
that	had	was	boy
in	if	come	three
not	some	get	down
for	up	or	work
at	her	two	put
with	do	man	were
it	when	little	before
on	so	has	just
can	my	them	long
will	very	how	here
are	all	like	other
of	would	our	old
this	any	what	take
your	been	know	cat
as	out	make	again
but	there	which	give
be	from	much	after
have	day	his	many

Instant (Sight) Words: Fry's Second 100 Words

saw	big	may	ran
home	where	let	five
soon	am	use	read
stand	ball	these	over
box	morning	right	such
upon	live	present	way
first	four	tell	too
came	last	next	shall
girl	color	please	own
house	away	leave	most
find	red	hand	sure
because	friend	more	thing
made	pretty	why	only
could	eat	better	near
book	want	under	than
look	year	while	open
mother	white	should	kind
run	got	never	must
school	play	each	high
people	found	best	far
night	left	another	both
into	men	seem	end
say	bring	tree	also
think	wish	name	until
back	black	dear	call

Instant (Sight) Words: Fry's Third 100 Words

ask	hat	off	fire
small	car	sister	ten
yellow	write	happy	order
show	try	once	part
goes	myself	didn't	early
clean	longer	set	fat
buy	those	round	third
thank	hold	dress	same
sleep	full	fell	love
letter	carry	wash	hear
jump	eight	start	yesterday
help	sing	always	eyes
fly	warm	anything	door
don't	sit	around	clothes
fast	dog	close	through
cold	ride	walk	o'clock
today	hot	money	second
does	grow	turn	water
face	cut	might	town
green	seven	hard	took
every	woman	along	pair
brown	funny	bed	now
coat	yes	fine	keep
six	ate	sat	head
gave	stop	hope	food

Reprinted with permission of Edward Fry, Ph.D., Laguna Beach Educational Books. From *The Reading Tutor's Handbook* by Jeanne Shay Schumm and Gerald E. Schumm Jr. Copyright ©1999. Free Spirit Publishing Inc., Minneapolis, MN, 1-800-735-7323, <www.freespirit.com>.
This page may be photocopied for individual, classroom, or group work only.

told	time	word	wear
Miss	yet	almost	Mr.
father	true	thought	side
children	above	send	poor
land	still	receive	lost
interest	meet	pay	outside
government	since	nothing	wind
feet	number	need	Mrs.
garden	state	mean	learn
done	matter	late	held
country	line	half	front
different	remember	fight	built
bad	large	enough	family
across	few	feel	began
yard	hit	during	air
winter	cover	gone	young
table	window	hundred	ago
story	even	week	world
sometimes	city	between	airplane
I'm	together	change	without
tried	sun	being	kill
horse	life	care	ready
something	street	answer	stay
brought	party	course	won't
shoes	suit	against	paper

continued ⟶

Instant (Sight) Words: Fry's Second 300 Words continued...

hour	grade	egg	spell
glad	brother	ground	beautiful
follow	remain	afternoon	sick
company	milk	feed	became
believe	several	boat	cry
begin	war	plan	finish
mind	able	question	catch
pass	charge	fish	floor
reach	either	return	stick
month	less	sir	great
point	train	fell	guess
rest	cost	hill	bridges
sent	evening	wood	church
talk	note	add	lady
went	past	ice	tomorrow
bank	room	chair	snow
ship	flew	watch	whom
business	office	alone	women
whole	cow	how	among
short	visit	arm	road
certain	wait	dinner	farm
fair	teacher	hair	cousin
reason	spring	service	bread
summer	picture	class	wrong
fill	bird	quite	age

continued ⟶

become	herself	demand	aunt
body	idea	however	system
chance	drop	figure	lie
act	river	case	cause
die	smile	increase	marry
real	son	enjoy	possible
speak	bat	rather	supply
already	fact	sound	thousand
doctor	sort	eleven	pen
step	king	music	condition
itself	dark	human	perhaps
nine	themselves	court	produce
baby	whose	force	twelve
minute	study	plant	rode
ring	fear	suppose	uncle
wrote	move	law	labor
happen	stood	husband	public
appear	himself	moment	consider
heart	strong	person	thus
swim	new	result	least
felt	often	continue	power
fourth	toward	price	mark
I'll	wonder	serve	president
kept	twenty	national	voice
well	important	wife	whether

Printing Chart: Zaner-Bloser Style

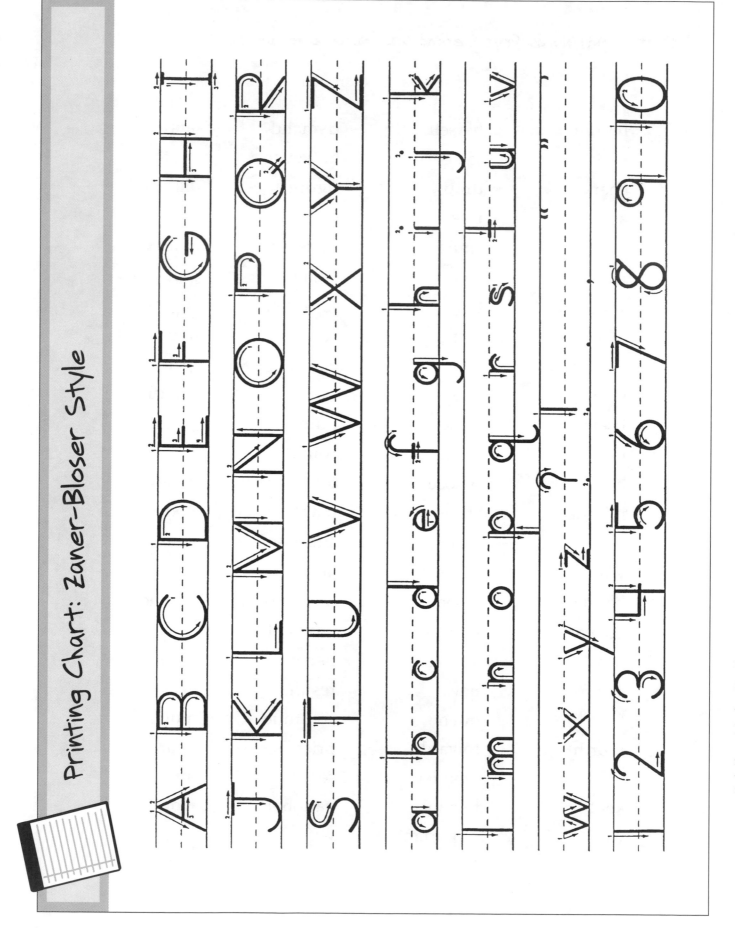

Printing Practice Paper

Cursive Chart: Zaner-Bloser Style

Used with permission from Zaner-Bloser, Inc. From *The Reading Tutor's Handbook* by Jeanne Shay Schumm and Gerald E. Schumm Jr. Copyright ©1999. Free Spirit Publishing Inc., Minneapolis, MN, 1-800-735-7323, <www.freespirit.com>. This page may be photocopied for individual, classroom, or group work only.

Cursive Practice Paper

	B	I	N	G	O
1					
2					
3			**FREE**		
4					
5					

			FREE		

GLOSSARY

"A-OK" method—one way to make revising easier and more efficient. (See page 96.)

Affiliated volunteers—unpaid tutors who are associated with a nonprofit organization (such as a church group, sorority or fraternity, or service organization).

At risk—vulnerable to having difficulties reading and writing and succeeding in school.

Blending—taking individual sounds and blending them into a word.

Book awareness—an understanding of what a book is and the basic parts of a book—cover, pages, title, etc.

Compound words—two shorter words put together to form a new work (for example: butterfly, cupboard).

Corporate volunteers—some businesses encourage employees to get involved in volunteer literacy efforts over and above their regular job responsibilities.

Dialogue journal—a book that you and your student can write together, in a conversational style.

Dysgraphia—a learning disability that involves severe problems in learning to write.

Dyslexia—a learning disability that involves severe problems in learning to read.

Environmental print awareness—refers to the ability to read familiar signs and symbols seen every day.

Expository writing—informational writing.

Frustration level—the grade level of material that students cannot read; even with help from a teacher, students cannot recognize most of the words and understanding of key ideas is very difficult.

Grammar and composition—includes instruction in the conventions of language (parts of speech, punctuation, mechanics) and in written communication in a variety of forms (short stories, essays, business and friendly letters, etc.).

Handwriting—includes instruction in both manuscript (print) and cursive (script).

Independent level—the grade level of material that students can read on their own; students know all the words and can read smoothly and understand fully.

Independent volunteers—unpaid tutors from the community who donate their time and effort to literacy initiatives.

Instructional level—the grade level of material that students can read with a little help from a teacher or tutor; students know most of the words (missing one or two here and there) and understand most of the key ideas.

Invented spellings—nonstandard spellings based on what children hear and also remember about the visual representation.

IEP—an Individualized Education Program. An IEP is an individualized instruction plan that has been approved by the student's parents as well as a committee of school district personnel.

Literature-centered programs—literacy programs that focus primarily on the read-aloud experience using trade books (or regular library books).

Literacy tutor—someone who coaches students—one at a time—in reading and writing. The literacy tutor provides both instruction and guidance and serves as a positive role model for her or his students.

Materials-centered programs—literacy programs for which individual publishers, professional organizations, and school districts have produced materials for volunteer and paid tutors.

Narrative writing—story writing.

Onset—detecting beginning sounds of words.

Paraprofessionals—adults who are paid to serve in support roles in school; they may be either part or full time, and are sometimes called teacher aids.

Phonics—refers to the teaching of sound/letter relationships.

Phonological awareness—the ability to hear sounds in words and detect differences in those sounds.

Print awareness—the skill of naming and differentiating the letters of the alphabet.

Professional-centered programs—literacy programs that rely less on materials and more on the judgment of a professional (special education teacher or reading specialist).

Readability level—the level of difficulty of reading material, usually reported as a grade level (for example, a fifth-grade readability level).

Reading comprehension—includes instruction in understanding an author's message (both literal and inferential) and in structuring a response or reaction to the author's message.

Rhyme—detecting ending sounds of words.

Schoolwork-centered programs—literacy programs in which students bring their homework to tutoring sessions and tutors provide help and assistance in completing assignments.

Segmentation—detecting the individual sounds of a whole word.

Service-learning students—middle school, high school, or college students who participate in literacy tutoring as part of a course or community service requirement.

Sight words—words that occur frequently in the English language and should be learned by "sight." Because these words occur so frequently, it is inefficient to take the time to "sound out" these words.

Spelling—the ability to write words according to standard conventions.

Story awareness—includes understanding of basic story structure.

Student workers—students who are paid to tutor, usually on an hourly basis.

TACT—a strategy to sensitively communicate information to parents and key stakeholders, in which a tutor can Tell something good about the student, Ask questions, Collaborate to identify areas of improvement, and Tie things together. (See page 117.)

TAG—a feedback system in which you Tell what you like, Ask questions, and Give suggestions. (See pages 102–103.)

Tutor-centered programs—literacy programs in which tutors assess student needs and select materials for remediation of those needs.

Vocabulary—refers to the knowledge of word meanings and concepts.

Word recognition—the ability to read individual words either in isolation or in context.

INDEX

ABOUT THE AUTHORS

Jeanne Shay Schumm, Ph.D., is a professor at the University of Miami in Coral Gables, Florida. She is also the chair of the Department of Teaching and Learning and teaches undergraduate and graduate courses in reading education. She is director of the university's Student Literacy Corps project, a volunteer tutoring program. Jeanne also serves as program evaluator for the Miami-Dade Public School's America Reads program. Her current research activities includes research and development of phonological awareness and reading comprehension strategies for young readers. She has coauthored *How to Help Your Child with Homework* and *School Power* with Marguerite Cogorno Radencich, Ph.D., as well as two college education textbooks.

Gerald E. Schumm Jr., D.Min., is an ordained minister serving a congregation at Coral Gables Congregational Church. He is a certified teacher with seven years of teaching experience at the elementary school level. An expert in volunteer enlistment and training, Jerry works with a number of volunteer projects including Habitat for Humanity, Daily Bread Food Bank, and Rotary International.

Jerry and Jeanne live at the Eaton Residential College on the University of Miami campus. They serve as faculty-in-residence at the college. They work together with college students in a variety of volunteer projects—including Miami America Reads and Habitat for Humanity.

OTHER GREAT BOOKS FROM FREE SPIRIT

How to Help Your Child with Homework
Every Caring Parent's Guide to Encouraging Good Study Habits and Ending the Homework Wars
by Marguerite C. Radencich, Ph.D., and Jeanne Shay Schumm, Ph.D.
Put an end to excuses and arguments while improving your child's school performance. Realistic strategies and proven techniques make homework hassle-free. Includes handouts, resources, and real-life examples. For parents of children ages 6–13.
$14.95; 208 pp.; softcover; 7¼" x 9¼"

School Power
Strategies for Succeeding in School
by Jeanne Shay Schumm, Ph.D., and Marguerite C. Radencich, Ph.D.
This book for school success covers everything students need to know, including how to get organized, take notes, study smarter, write better, follow directions, handle homework, and more. For ages 11 & up.
$13.95; 132 pp.; softcover; B&W photos and illus.; 8½" x 11"

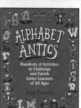

Alphabet Antics
Hundreds of Activities to Challenge and Enrich Letter Learners of All Ages
written and illustrated by Ken Vinton, M.A.
This fresh, inventive approach to the ABCs promotes creativity, stimulates curiosity, and invites exploration and discovery through activities and illustrated, reproducible handouts. For grades K–6.
$19.95; 144 pp.; softcover; illus.; 8½" x 11"

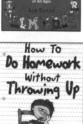

How to Do Homework Without Throwing Up
written and illustrated by Trevor Romain
"Everybody who goes to school does homework…and they feel just as sick as you do when they have to do it." Trevor Romain understands how horrible homework can be. Kids will recognize this right away—and as they laugh along with Trevor's jokes, they'll learn how to make a homework schedule, when to do the hardest homework (first!), where to do homework, the benefits of homework, and more. For ages 8–13.
$8.95; 72 pp.; softcover; illus.; 5⅛" x 7"

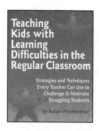

Teaching Kids with Learning Difficulties in the Regular Classroom
Strategies and Techniques Every Teacher Can Use to Challenge & Motivate Struggling Students
by Susan Winebrenner
Proven, practical teaching methods, strategies, and techniques for meeting the needs of special education students, those labeled "slow" or "remedial," and all others who struggle to learn in the mixed-abilities classroom. For teachers, all grades.
$27.95; 248 pp.; softcover; 8½" x 11"

To place an order or to request a free catalog of SELF–HELP FOR KIDS® and SELF–HELP FOR TEENS® materials, please write, call, email, or visit our Web site:

Free Spirit Publishing Inc.
400 First Avenue North • Suite 616 • Minneapolis, MN 55401-1724
toll-free 800.735.7323 • local 612.338.2068 • fax 612.337.5050
help4kids@freespirit.com • www.freespirit.com